WHAT MATTERS MOST:
FAMILY, FRIENDS, AND FOES

WHAT MATTERS MOST: FAMILY, FRIENDS, AND FOES

Owen Watson

Library of Congress Control Number:		2015919074
ISBN:	Hardcover	978-1-5144-2727-9
	Softcover	978-1-5144-2726-2
	eBook	978-1-5144-2725-5

Print information available on the last page.

Rev. date: 11/19/2015

To order additional copies of this book, contact:
Xlibris
1-888-795-4274
www.Xlibris.com
Orders@Xlibris.com
727532

CONTENTS

FOREWORD

WHAT MATTERS MOST: Family, Friends, and Foes is the realization of a dream that the author and my husband (Owen) has had in his heart for the past sixty years that I've known him. Just kidding! However, this project is the culmination of some of the more impactful and salient events in his life being shared in an effort to be an encouragement to any and all who would read its content. In reality, ever since I've known him, he maintains a mission to uplift and encourage others around him . . . a characteristic that I believe is both inspired by God and a reflection of his gratefulness to God for all that he has been blessed and entrusted with.

This book is one that you can almost refer to as you would a devotional. I say this because it is not the type that is "digested" in one reading. The inspirational quotes, poems, and philosophies that are part of the book will probably be referred to over and over again or possibly at key times when they may speak to a particular situation that you are facing. In either case, *What Matters Most: Family, Friends, and Foes* is meant to inspire, motivate, and challenge you to view circumstances in your life and those that God allows into it (family, friends, or foes) as opportunities for personal growth, cultivating your gifts, and helping to improve the lives of others! You were placed here to make an impact, and only you can determine what type of impact that will be. Enjoy the journey!

Dr. Ramona L. Watson

ACKNOWLEDGMENTS

S PECIAL THANKS TO the following:

Ramona – A wonderful inspiration as my wife and partner, who makes me laugh, pushes me when necessary, and comforts me in times of overexertion. You are my God-given life mate and well worth the wait. I love you completely!

Aubrian – An ideal son above any I could've ever dreamed of having. May your adventurous spirit continue to be fulfilled beyond limitations and according to your faith in Him. Thank you so much for being an inspiration to me and a part of my everyday joy. Love you much!

Audrianna – A treasure, a jewel is what you are to me. Full of joy and laughter, you are God's prescription to what this world lacks. Such a tender heart and caring person; thanks for uplifting me through our many conversations and silly antics with one another. Love you much!

Tommy (father) – My guide and who I reflect in going the extra mile for others. A man of faith in action beyond mere words; you have laid the path well that allowed me to serve a broader audience. You are forever a part of all I do and will always remain cherished within my heart. Love you much!

Leamorica (mother) – My rock, my confidant, my biggest supporter through all things! Neither written words nor expressed deeds could ever show the depth of appreciation I have for you. We've shared many talks, trips, joyous moments, and sad occasions; and through it all, we've still entrusted everything in His hands for the good. Whereas others made up pieces of me, you have been the biggest part of me. Love you immeasurably!

Pleamon (father-in-law) and Shirley (mother-in-law) – I could not have married into a better family! You've accepted and treated me as a son from day 1 and have found me "fit for duty" to wed your beautiful daughter—a queen she is! Love you both dearly and am looking forward to many more family trips, good eating, and memorable occasions to partake of.

Dr. Kelvin Richardson – My dearest friend and mentor. Thanks for all the wisdom you've imparted in me, along with the brotherhood that we share. You are truly an inspiration. Much love, bro!

Vincent Smith – My friend, my brother, my mentor. Too many laughs to mention, yet none will ever be forgotten. Thanks for "reeling" me back in the faith. The effects of your friendship and joy have been unbelievably nurturing throughout all levels of my life. Much love, bro!

Chris Marshall – God's workman, my friend, my mentor. The man who prophesied that I would leave the military within a month and work at the U.S. Postal Service for a season—wow! It really did happen. The man who continues to bless my wife and me in too many ways to mention. Nothing but much love, bro!

Teresa Allen – God's woman, my friend! Always there for me and with me during some tumultuous times—a dedicated comrade and prayer warrior. Forever friends . . . Much love!

Ptr. Charles Warman – My first true pastor as an adult, my friend. Great memories we shared in doing the Lord's work. I am truly thankful for your teaching and presenting opportunities to me as an entrusted minister. Much love, Pastor!

Ptr. Lenard Hardaway – Man of faith, my friend, my mentor. Loads of fun, ministry and personal development, opportunities, and support you have provided with a genuine heart. I am forever grateful for our connection as friends above all. Much love, Pastor!

Ptr. Thomas McGhee – Man of God, my friend, my mentor. Really am missing your teaching and our Tuesday lunch group on base. I've learned so much from you that I carry with me every day. Eternally grateful for our friendship and brotherhood in faith. Much love, Pastor!

CMDCM Glenn Hopkins (retired) – My friend, the "Big Guy!" Never shall I forget your mentorship and the immeasurable opportunities you have afforded me.

I would also like to acknowledge the following persons for their significant impressions in my life and career: Nikita Allen-Honorable, Mark Baker, Rick and Eulonda Banks, Craig Beasley, Lucretia Benson, Patricia Billups, Princeton Blanchard, Shontay Bond, Barbara Booth, Colonel Dawn Brotherton, Dr. Michael Brown, Elder Robert Brown, Ptr. Joey Buran, Sharita Burns, Terence Burton, Rosie Callicott, Linda Calloway, Paige Chaffen, Byron Clemmons, Lawrence Collins,

Michael Collins, Wandra Cosby, CMDCM Jeffrey Covington, Irma Currington, Karl Darr, Lunden Davis, Frank Denkins, Sam Desta, Alice "LC" DeStasio-Brickhouse, Gary and Sylvia Dixon, LTC Leigh Ann Erdman, Walter Ezell, Elizabeth Fisher, Antonio Ford, Dave Feser, Brenda Fuentes, Shiann Fuentes, Sierra Fuentes, James Furlow, Dianne Galloway, April Garcia, Natasha Garrett, Michael Griffin, Randy Hall, Donna Hardaway, Erius Hardaway, Ora Hardaway, Jermaine Henry, Travis Hogan, Kaelen Howard, Tondalaya Henry, Elijah and Anna Jones, Gregory Jones, Cory Jordan, Jeri "TC" Kincade, JTF-CS family, James Kotrch, Raymond Larry, Jr., Denise Lark, Sharon Lark, Frederick Lewis, Mark Lofton, Jason Lohr, Kenneth Lucas, Darren Lucas, Stacie Madkins, Maj. Gen. (ret) Jeff Mathis, Pastor Kenneth and Cynthia McPherson, Brent Middleton, Beth Miller, Beverly Miller, Frederick Mitchell, Minnie Mitchell-Kline, Antonio Myles, Diana Pegeuese, Captain Andrea Petrovanie, Brenda Rainey, Callie Rainey, Classy Rainey, Harold Rainey, Karl Rainey, Kerrie Rainey, Thomas Rainey, DeLove Redd, Rene Retterer, Marie Roland, Jason Roth, Maj. Gen. and Mrs. Roy, Steven Schoenleber, Margaret Smith, Albert and Lillie Staten, Brigette Stevenson, Tommy Sr. and Annie Stevenson, Tommy Stevenson, Jr., Cathy Thomas, Capt. (ret) Eric Tibbetts, Maj. Gen. (ret) Jonathan Treacy, Mark Wallace, Adm. (ret) Patrick Walsh, Diamond Watson, Hartzell Watson, Maurice Watson, Otis Watson, Andre Welch, Overseer Medris Wellington, Kevin Wells, Carol White, Bo Wittington, Stevean Wischoff, Capt. (ret) Craig Wilson, and Corey and Tomorra Young.

INTRODUCTION

I T'S BEEN WHISPERED to me over the past five to ten years that I should write a book to encourage others because of what was known of my personal situations and hiccups in life. So when the appropriate time presented itself, along with peace in spirit to do so, I decided to go for it, and here we are with the birth of *What Matters Most: Family, Friends, and Foes.* This is not a publication to solicit sorrow or remorse but to share in life's ups and downs while steadily pressing forward with your faculties intact. I believe the primary key to succeeding in life is God; second to that, I attribute to people we encounter throughout our lives, whether they are family, friends, or foes.

Typically, family and friends are your champions for success; however, they can also portray the characteristics of a foe along with the already positioned foes. Nevertheless, should we dare to discard the negative and only accept the positive? In this day and age, it sounds strange and unnerving, huh? Well, it is so often easy to accept the positive, but what if there is viable reason for us to accept the negative responses as well? What if the purpose of those negative responses were to serve as calibration tools to help define, refine, and guide us to something larger beyond the "it's about me" world? Your response to those negative responses says more about you than it does of those whom you believe are against you.

What Matters Most: Family, Friends, and Foes offers a dissecting look at a culmination of everyday people from diverse backgrounds through various circumstances and realizes the impacts they have had on my life with regard to who and where I am today. Whether deemed as "good or bad," indifferent, or simply insignificant, there is something in everyone who crosses our path in life that we can either learn from or be grateful for. For instance, someone who may have criticized you because of your lack of education may also be the fuel you needed to revive that ambition and press forward in getting that alluded degree. Henceforth, that critical someone has just indirectly but positively impacted you in achieving something you may have otherwise not have given a second thought of doing. Now by having that degree, it becomes a stepping stone for you entering into a door broadened with opportunities.

We each bring something to the table in this life; the key is looking beyond the emotional connections or disconnections and laying hold of the value—that being either the reason or impact that person has had in your life. All our hopes and dreams are tied to the audience of family, friends, and foes based on impacts they have imparted into our lives. There have been many times where I have had to just sit back and smile when someone has wronged me. This I have done knowing that it was a learning experience designed not to harm me but to better me in my dealings with certain people. That aspect of thinking has personally saved me from many headaches.

Just like the aforementioned example of how criticism can serve to ignite a fire in you, so are many other illustrations within *What Matters Most: Family, Friends, and Foes*, through a biographical snippet of my life experiences. I write this book with the intent to encourage and inspire you not to give up on your dreams, not to harbor bitterness against others, and to provide hope in living beyond the denials, hurts, loneliness, and misunderstandings that others may have caused in your life.

What matters most about those family, friends, and foes? Keep reading, and you'll be sure to find something relatively inspiring to you beyond your today.

OWEN WATSON

SECTION 1

Something More in Life

WHAT'S MORE IN life is your very existence! God has allowed each of us to be here to make one another better in some form or another. Regardless of the situation, whether good or bad, there is something positive that can be learned from it all. When we trade our "sunglasses" for His "Son-glasses," we can begin to appreciate the guidance He is giving us in life, especially through family, friends, and foes. If we stand firm in His presence, His will; and in knowing that all things will work in our favor, we can then develop a whole new perspective on our daily interactions with whomever—yes, even your supposed enemy.

Be motivated by family, friends, and foes!

CHAPTER 1

Dodge the Rock, Catch the Nugget

IN 1980 WHILE growing up in Chicago (Englewood) at the age of ten, having to walk three blocks home from a makeshift trailer park school located in Hermitage Park wasn't always much of an enjoyable venture, especially when some of those times included teenagers throwing rocks at you from afar. Oddly, my buddy and I found ourselves to be frequent targets of their devious deeds. Although the rocks never made their mark on me, my buddy was not as fortunate—having to receive seventeen stitches slightly above his left temple. Bizarrely, they found it amusing, but my internal thoughts at such an early age were filled with sorrow for my buddy and pity for them.

As I reflect back on the situation, I believe the pity I derived came from knowing their status of being high school dropouts, primarily serving no purpose other than to make life miserable for others, just as the old adage goes, "Misery loves company." Often, you would see them in assemblies along the streets and underneath viaducts looking for victims to harass. The younger boys and girls were the preferred targets for harassment, while the elderly were the preferred targets for robbing. Nevertheless, their wrongdoings during that time seem to pale in comparison to those of today's juveniles—it now appears as though it can't get any worse! Regardless, I doubt if any of the victims would find it "better" in either case.

Rather than telling my parents about the situation, I just kept it to myself, dodged the rocks when necessary, and altered my travel routes to avoid contact. As we say in the navy, I just "carried on smartly." It was a doable plan of action that paid off for me but not so much for my buddy. Where he lived, he had no choice but to continue on the same route and endure the offences. He was part of a single-parent home consisting of his mom and younger brother. His mother was aware of the happenings, but unfortunately, she really couldn't do too much to mitigate the circumstances because of working various jobs.

Enduring this type of experience from an early age can surely have an effect on one's outlook on life. It can either break or make you. Unfortunately, many succumb to such environments as simply a way of life, leading to hopelessness. Through the eyes of a child, it can begin as fear that eventually transforms to desensitized complacency. From there, the unacceptable environment often becomes much broader with the addition of another generation.

For those of us who had refused to give in, life wasn't made any easier, but we were naively made much stronger, committed, and determined to overcome obstacles and dream bigger. For me, the more I observed the rampant juvenile behaviors, the more I became stirred to learn, do, and live better from the illustration I saw in my parents. So instead of the street loiters having a negative influence on me, I credit them for showing me what not to become. No one has to repeat vile and unbefitting conduct that is blatantly obvious in the life of someone else.

As I stated earlier, I had developed pity for all of them. It's easy to make blanket judgments against anyone, but it's difficult to ignore the truth you know about someone. Many came from various difficult backgrounds, never having been loved or knowing how to love. Additionally, with very little education, they also lacked in social skills. For some, they attended school, but it wasn't long before they ended up obtaining their "education" from the streets instead. Ironically, I witnessed both teachers and students recklessly contributing to these fragile young prospects becoming societal rejects. When they did go to school, they were put to shame by other students and some teachers, with things ranging from how they dressed to how they communicated to how they looked and on and on. Such rejection served as fuel for their choosing to live someplace where they felt they could be accepted without judgment . . . the streets.

Respectful Relationships

During our time of living in the Englewood area of Chicago from the early 1970s to 1981, we have had some of the best times as the community occasionally came together for a neighborhood block party. Under the leadership of my father, you would see people of all ages, races, and backgrounds within a six-block radius walking the streets in droves picking up trash, providing lawn services, painting, and cleaning throughout the neighborhood—all free of charge. To cap it all off, around noontime, some of the streets were allowed to be closed off from through traffic to allow for the setup of live bands playing the latest tracks. I tell you, there is nothing like observing pure raw and synchronized talent firsthand. Furthermore, there were tons of various foods for everyone as much as anyone wanted—again, all free of charge. As a young guy, all I could think was "What a heavenly experience this is!" It exemplified the epitome of a family-oriented community working together.

Coordinating such an event takes not only a leader but also the trusted company of dependable persons. Among those whom my father deemed trustworthy were a neighbor and friend whom I'll call Stephon. Stephon was energetic, enthusiastic, well known, and respected within the community; and the kids viewed him as the embodiment of "cool." He was also known as the neighborhood watchman, always keeping his "ears to the ground." He frequented our home so much that my siblings and I considered him as an uncle.

Moving forward, after living long enough, you reluctantly come to realize that all good things must come to an end. Well, sadly this community event was heading in that direction. Going back to the winter of 1980, as I was doing my after-school physical education in the form of running to dodge rocks, I remember noticing a strong smell of smoke as I approached the alley near my home (considered the "safe zone" from the rock throwers). Gathering myself together so that my appearance didn't give away that I was hiding something, I slowly proceeded to the corner of the street where I'd lived. As I approached the corner, I then noticed the area down near my home was blocked off by the fire department and police while loads of people were gathered around. As I made my way closer, there it was—the first shock of my entire life—our house was on fire!

One of the neighbors had my younger brother and me sit on their porch until either my parents or other siblings came. I tell you, it was the most eerie feeling I have ever felt! Many thoughts crossed my mind as to what could have happened to cause this devastation. The thoughts ranged from one of my brothers trying to boil a hot dog to a television or radio being left on and somehow sparking an electrical fire. When I say for an eleven-year-old that my nerves were shot, I mean I was completely mentally disturbed by this event. All of a sudden, I see a recognizable person rushing over to my younger brother and me—it was my mom. She first hugged me and my younger brother and then held our hands as our remaining three siblings joined us. What a sigh of relief to see them all unharmed! Shortly afterward, my father arrived, and there we were, all safe but saddened about the house. Unfortunately, certain rooms within the house were destroyed by the fire.

While awaiting the house to be reconstructed, we moved in with relatives for the time being. I must say that although we were grateful for the family support, there was still no place like being in your own home. A month had now passed since the fire occurred when we received word that it was not an accident but arson. Someone had thrown a couple of "cocktail" bombs through the kitchen window but somehow managed to sneak in prior and steal a couple of key items. Word going around the neighborhood was that the culprit was Stephon who frequently visited with us and helped coordinate the community block party events. What a shocking revelation—coincidentally, he was nowhere to be found or ever seen again after the incident.

There are those who come in peace with good intentions but slowly begin developing ulterior motives through envy of how comfortable your life is perceived to be in comparison to theirs. The teaching from such moments is not that you harbor resentment, lose trust in people, or become suspect of everyone who crosses your path but that you meet them where they are. Pay close attention to what they speak on the most; every so often, they will carelessly send you signals as to what areas of your relationship are caution areas, what areas need a "patrolled boarder," and what areas are safe, open-boarders. Just as my parents were, so should we all be—forgiving toward the supposed culprit and thankful that no lives were lost or personal injuries incurred. What matters most aren't those material things which can easily be replaced but respecting those relationships through close observation of the telltale communication signs.

Culture Shock

My father's mother (my grandmother) and stepfather (whom I forever consider my grandfather) lived in a small town called Blytheville, Arkansas. As a child, the only thing I have ever known about the place is that my older brother and I loved to go there during summer breaks to have a little freedom of exploration. We pretty much would be what many call "spoiled." It was fun being the new face in town, having young girls liking you and young guys wanting to hang around you as though you were a celebrity. It was a peaceful place with the only gunfire heard being at the hands of my grandmother shooting in the air at night whenever strange noises were heard outside the house, primarily perpetrated by raccoons. Looking back, I can remember when the first tar streets overlaid the dirt roads in the middle to late 1970s—particularly Jackson, Basin, Stuart, and Twenty-First Street.

Blytheville had become a town full of "firsts" for me to include learning how to climb a tree and having a "girlfriend." It was also a place where I first learned about gardening with my grandfather, something I really didn't care for because of my fear of certain "critters" and snakes. However, he had a way of encouraging me to get in there and handle business; it was called no work, no eat. My grandmother was one of the best cooks around and was known as being a woman of courage, strength, and fun. To this day, I believe my father and I inherited her work characteristics because she was one who refused to be held down by anything or anyone.

So then, during the summer of 1981, little did I know that our time of living and knowing Chicago as home was slowly but surely coming to an end. From the time we moved back into our home until midsummer, the neighborhood suffered many changes for the worse. Numerous neighboring families had moved out, being replaced by a much less mature crowd of people. The community as a whole had also begun to experience an acceleration of criminal activities and gang violence coupled with rapid gunfire throughout the nights. Moreover, my father's canary yellow 1971 Lincoln Continental was the target of many garage break-ins, so much so that he and my mother took turns keeping watch over the garage with the local police on speed dial.

With the environment becoming nonconducive to the way of life that my parents had hoped and worked for and the neighborhood beginning to attract more violence, my parents made the drastic decision of moving the family to Blytheville, Arkansas. This decision, as was told to me later on in life, was to afford me and my siblings the opportunity for a better future beyond what was being offered in Englewood as the gangs and infestation of drugs became more of an occurrence. Personally, I was happy with the decision because it meant going somewhere I was familiar with and spending more time with my grandparents. However, that happiness wouldn't last long when the beginning of the new school year came, and I had to meet new friends.

As I reflect on the entire situation from the house fire to the changing of the neighborhood to the move to Arkansas, as a person of faith, I can now see God was at work. Although at the time we might not know of Him or have the relationship we should with Him, He still sets the stage of opportunity for the better. The same can be said of anyone dealing with a turbulent situation. The key is not to cave in to the "impossibility" mind-set established as the norm by the apathetic but for us to be pliable and maintain a will, dream, and trust that God is working inside and outside the box on our behalf. His positioning is simply His way of creating networks in your life that will be valuable sources for use later.

What matters most during this section are the foes being voluntarily used by the enemy to force a move according to God's plan. No one can lay ahold of the more significant things of God if the insignificant things of man are more important within their hearts. Godly moves require faith, and unfortunately, sometimes this "faith" is usually executed without our realizing what and why we're doing what we do. Interestingly, when we do come to "know" God, we then try to figure out how "faith" works instead of just following as before.

TIE-IN INSPIRATIONS

~There is a voice of reasoning within each of us that simply says you have the means to move out from among the depressive environment—they're called faith, will, and a commitment to do what is right.

~One thing for certain, resistance can only be overcome by pressing forward—shake off the "norm" and walk in the "change"—you'll never know the greater that God has for you if you continually accept whatever the enemy is giving you!

~Your love for anything or anyone above God allows the enemy to be whatever you need him to be (even by using the word of God better than most) just to keep your faith misdirected and your God-designed purpose abandoned—ultimately, turning many form attempting to have faith in God and to a life of emptiness, regret, and bitterness.

~Having a will to learn is a goal; willing to learn is a start, but willingly learning shows progress. You can only do better when your will is put into action, challenging your thoughts to produce results!

~Do not complain about your nightmares when you've never made use of the tools God has given you to manifest your dreams.

~When you begin to realize that God allow others to get under your skin simply as a thermometer to measure where He is in your life, you will begin to pay less attention to their actions and give more attention to your purpose!

~Returning to where and what God has delivered you from is evidence of where your true love lies. Thankfully, God is still willing to deliver you again, for as long as it takes, based on His true love for each of us—however, what's at stake is our level of purposed potential having a deteriorated effectiveness!

CHAPTER 2

Look 'Em in the Eyes

L IVING IN BLYTHEVILLE, Arkansas, during the early 1980s was an experience that, even if I could, I wouldn't change for anything. For the most part, kids were able to be kids. You could play football in the streets, softball in the school parks or an empty school parking (like at Robinson Elementary), and anxiously appreciate and look forward to swinging, see-sawing, and sliding in the park with other children throughout the community. My pastime activity was gathering a couple of buddies to go and collect bottles, pecans, and tin cans to sell. As I learned from an uncle of mine, "always keep something in your pocket"—and it still pays off today. Back then, we took full advantage of being outside into evening hours playing all sorts of games such as hide-and-seek, jump rope, hop-scotch, bike riding, and, of course, "tag."

Many of us didn't mind sharing what we had with others that were without. However, there was a small pocket of bullies that had to be dealt with occasionally for wanting to take instead of asking. Truthfully, they were bitter individuals who only found happiness by dampening the fun for others. Anyway, there were ways as a kid that you could actually go out and make a couple of dollars easily, and you were satisfied with the money you would've made. What I would do is make whatever money I could, go buy loads of candy, and take it to school to sell to kids who lived out in rural areas without the candy stores. We practically had one on every corner in the city.

It wasn't until my grandfather taught me that I learned a little something about business. Rule number one, as he explained, was "never sell for the same price you paid." The reason being is that you took the time to walk and buy the goodies with them in mind, when you could've done something else for yourself in that time. Made sense, note taken!

His final rule number two, as he continued, was "never let them talk you down from the price you've set—look 'em in the eyes and stand firm." Humorously speaking, that rule only worked sometimes for me because oftentimes they were much bigger than me, and I was persuaded to settle for a smaller profit. Nonetheless, at that time, I didn't grasp the concept of "looking them in the eye" and why that was a part of the rule. After all, my concern was more on needing to use my eyes in counting them out the correct number of pieces of candy. Before long, I would come to learn the importance of looking them in the eyes.

Getting the Job

Around the time I reached the age of fifteen, the candy business was starting to take a turn because of stiff competition from others in the neighborhood who found a "cheaper" way to acquire candy and sell it for half the price that I would've paid for it at the store. With this tapping into my bottom-line method of making profits, I had to think of other ways to make better money.

Riding my bicycle one day along with my buddy James, I noticed a person throwing newspapers from their car and was struck with an idea; yes, I could become a paperboy! Over the next couple of days, because of my parents being at work, I solicited my uncle for taking me to the local newspaper carrier's office for a job interview to become a paperboy.

As we were riding, he began practicing interview questions with me before abruptly pulling over on the side of the road. Not sure of what the problem was, I asked was everything all right. He looks at me and says, "No." I'm thinking I hadn't answered one of the questions satisfactory, but it was something more than that. In a stern voice, he orders me to look at him in the eye. He proceeded to explain that when talking to anyone, do not look in any other direction besides into the person's eyes whom you are addressing.

Suddenly, the voice of my grandfather began to ring in my thoughts: "Look 'em in the eye." This time I was going to find out why that was so important, so I proceeded to ask him. He quickly smartened me up about how you physically position yourself in addressing someone is just as important as your verbal response; it all boils down to respect, honesty, and integrity. Lesson learned and well-received. As it turned out, putting that short lesson into practice got me my first job.

Paying the Price

Although I had gotten the job, it didn't quite last as long as I would've liked. Even though this was my first official job and one that I had enjoyed, it only lasted for about one month. The story goes like this: Payment for the papers was due biweekly. I was tasked with collecting the payments and turning them into the office finance person. Well, knowing that my pay was going to be $54, I decided to take it out of the money I had collected from the customers, not thinking of it as being a big deal; oh, how wrong I was.

Coming home one day from completing the distribution of papers, my father and mother were in the kitchen on the phone. As you could probably guess, yes, it was with the newspaper office.

Long story short, the funds I turned in were $54 shorter than expected, and they wanted to know if I may have mistakenly lost or misplaced it. Well, at this time, I had some explaining to do. My mother began with the words, "Look me in the eyes and tell us what actually happened." As I explained the complete story to her and my father, they expressed their disappointment, and my father paid the debt on my behalf; however, my punishment was to quit the job and work off the debt by cutting the lawns of people at the church. What a relief and difference looking someone in the eyes with the truth can make.

Given our nature, we as people are prone to resist doing new things, especially if they tend to make us feel uncomfortable. God positions people in our life to help break down the walls of self-security and to expose us to discipline for our growth. Knowing that no one person has all the answers, we can then begin to accept God's answers through anyone. Just as the lesson for me to "look 'em in the eyes" was worthwhile in securing me a job and avoiding grievous discipline, it can be useful too when we spiritually look God in the eye for His favor upon us in life.

TIE-IN INSPIRATIONS

~Freedom begins with knowledge and ends with revelation—knowing the Author exposes the destiny you've been reborn for!

~The joy of family begins when you recognize our importance in God's plan for the family! Quality is beyond gift giving; it entails learning each other and discussing/developing ways to inspire one another in being the positively best wherever you're positioned in life!

~As you gradually reach higher altitudes in life, what matters most is conservation of air—make sure every spoken word counts for something!

~Serving God isn't about what we can get but how and what He wants to provide for others through us. The favor of God in our lives is evident in how we positively impact the lives of others!

~Seven Measures of Success

♦ A measure of one's honesty is evident in one's relationships.
♦ A measure of one's faith is evident in one's determination.
♦ A measure of one's holiness is evident in one's position in making positive differences for others.
♦ A measure of one's trustworthiness is evident in one's choice to discard gossip.
♦ A measure of one's humbleness is evident in one putting others first without an ulterior motive of personal gain.
♦ A measure of one's prosperity is evident in one's peace and patience.
♦ A measure of one's love is evident in whom one is ultimately accountable to.

CHAPTER 3

Turning the Page

S O OFTEN WE as people subliminally tend to differentiate between who, why, and how someone is deemed "better" than ourselves. Whether it's what someone has, how they look, what they wear, or even how they speak, a sense of esteemed value causes divisions resulting in either negative or positive responses. Depending on who's delivering the response, it creates an even further breakdown resulting in separation. These types of separations are likely to hinder relationships of all types and produce callous feelings toward people whom we may know nothing about; the end result becomes the fabrication of prejudices, low self-esteem, mistreatment of certain people, and lack of afforded opportunities.

Part of our maturing in life comes when we're able to accept people as viable individuals despite the indifferences. Our understanding must expand to the point of realizing that everyone brings something to the table of life, even those whom are truly out to bring harm our way. Truth is, what hinders many of us from reaching beyond our potential is our lack of or misuse of faith. We haphazardly use our faith to support our false beliefs rather than for what it was intended to do. Of course, as aforementioned, some of us do this regularly in how we subliminally judge people who may actually be the missing link of getting us where God would have us to be.

While I was working in Millington, I was frequently maintaining a positive spirit without realizing that I was holding back on my potential. See, I would always give compliments on how certain people were very smart, how some were the "go-to" people or how sharp some appeared in uniform. Although there was nothing in itself wrong with what I was doing and it was creating a positive effect on people's "ego," I hadn't realized how I was stunting the growth of my own abilities and potential. If it had not been caught soon enough, this sort of behavior could have led to me receiving poor performance evaluations because of my confidence in what others could do rather than what I was capable of doing.

It wasn't until I met this officer—now known as Dr. Richardson—who overheard me complimenting someone on how "smart" they were for answering what I thought to be a difficult question about dealing with the job—that this changed. He pulled me to the side and asked, "Why do you label that person as being smart?" I respectfully replied, "Because he had the answer to a problem I was faced with." Then I heard the words that would change not only how I interacted with others but my performance as well. He sat me down and said, "The only thing that makes anyone smarter than anyone else is simply them turning the page."

Those words spoke volumes as they resonated within me. They were so full of truth and pertain practically to anything we do in life, whether it is knowledge, how we look or feel, or how we may become the "go-to" person. For me, that was a God-sent word that I immediately began to share with others during Bible studies and general counseling sessions with junior personnel.

By turning the page, we can begin to eradicate prejudices and jealousies. We start to fulfill our purpose by exercising the potential within us, coupled with the measure of faith He has allotted to each of us. In doing so, we can spend time on building our record of reliability and matters that pertain to us while still helping others and not diminishing the worth of our own talents. Knowledge is only powerful when it is acted upon; however, in order to move forward in action, it has to be fueled by a "faith"-filled purpose.

Turning the page was also illustrated to me in regard to another situation. When I reported to a new unit, I asked this very nice lady, "How is it working with the people throughout the unit?" Her response was a little startling; she basically responded with "judge for yourself." That was it; nothing more, nothing less. Again, in essence, she was simply saying to turn the page and find out by reaching out; don't get stuck in your comfort zone, and don't allow anyone to set prejudices in your mind about someone else. That was advice that served me well to know because so often we formulate negative opinions based on what others say when our own personal interactions may prove to be quite different.

A good buddy of mine named Gary served as evidence of turning the page in his life as many of us do when we truly welcome God in. I remember first meeting this guy and seeing a lot of myself in him by how he would tell the most hilarious stories using profanity to the utmost. Of course, his profanity was more polished compared to some of the words I'd used or shall I say misused—I'll just say he was pretty seasoned.

Anyway, when I received an invite to come witness he and his wife dedicate their lives to God, I was sort of torn between being ecstatic and distraught. Spiritually, I was ecstatic because of this great life-changing event that was being witnessed by friends and family who knew life with them before. However, I was distraught because I knew this would mean an end to hearing some of those funny, cuss-filled stories—that was the flesh side of me! In all seriousness, this brother has been such an instrument used by God not only in my life but also in the lives of countless others—he was also the best man at my wedding.

Turning the page isn't always something that is easy to do, but it can be done. It's something that we each have the measure of faith and choice to do. It's never too late to look beyond yesterday and/or today. Gradual efforts produce whole results that can benefit all. Your legacy can be viewed as a content dependence on others or a "system"; or it can be fulfilling in knowing you've made a positive contributory impact to society. Don't be one who is capable of making a change yet chooses to forfeit faith and efforts for the sake of just being alive—refusing to turn the page.

TIE-IN INSPIRATIONS

-Do you remember you once dreamed of being someone great? Well, that dream became a reality the moment you gave your life to God and accepted becoming a new creation—your purpose is of a higher calling far greater than what you previously lived for!

-You can waste so much time being frustrated, trying to make something happen, or become something that's not in God's plan for you. Yet many will not let go because they have it in their heart to prove something to others rather than obey God. Your sacrifice leaves God with the broken down leftovers to work with, whereas your obedience allows Him to fully maximize all that is within you for something greater to be accomplished!

-Most resolutions can be achieved simply by accepting God's plan rather than one's own!

-Achieving what you're hoping for requires time, efforts, and commitment beyond what you give toward your everyday needs.

-God wittingly smiles when He asks us to give up something small, and we pant and make excuses, not knowing that He has something greater to give in return!

-Without a doubt, there are many least known children of God being used more than there are of the prominently known. The only witness you need is God, and the only testimony you need is how you've ministered to others without tooting your own horn or looking for recompense.

CHAPTER 4

Opportunities

WHILE LIVING IN Blytheville, Arkansas, soon after my honorable discharge from active duty with the U.S. Navy and securing a job with the Postal Service, I recall being in spiritual limbo. For whatever reason, I just could not figure out the next move in bringing peace to my spiritual life. After all, I had previously had the friendships of many throughout the years while in the navy, and now I was faced with what I now consider to have been a "tested moment of truth." At first, my family and I, along with a friend who moved there with us, began having small group Bible studies with no more than two to three people showing; although it was decent, it wasn't satisfying. It was not the amount of people showing or anxiety, but I believe it was not in God's plan at the time. So after a few weeks of doing the study group, it was disbanded.

Now we were faced with a decision of finding a local church home, although I wasn't too keen on the idea because of preferring the church environment I'd become accustomed to during my transformation in Virginia. One Sunday afternoon, when I arrived home from work at the Postal Service, my wife at that time and her friend came to me, excitedly telling me of this church called Revival Center that represented all backgrounds of people and had sound teaching accordingly. The following Sunday, I was there on the front pew. There was this former marine by the name of Pastor Warman who stood up and delivered a powerful message called "Where's Jesus?" Right then, I was impressed with a spiritual peace that this was where we should be.

During the next five years of being there, I was afforded the opportunity to preach, administer some special programs, help with the maintenance of the building, and, most importantly, meet and develop close relationships with almost everyone that was a member there. Many of them I still keep in contact with via online social media. Being there was a stripping and equipping stage in my life, a part of the format that I believe many who seek Him must accept and understand.

As time went on, the inevitable had taken place—9/11. In the midst of the United States responding by sending forces over to Iraq, as a selective reservist, I was being recalled to active duty in the U.S. Navy at Millington, Tennessee. My assignment was to assist in forming a Mobilization Augmentation center that provided full support and tracking of all navy reservists being recalled. I would've never believed it had I not witnessed it for myself, the amount of people of all ages calling to volunteer their services for being recalled. For sure, one thing I recognized by being there was that there are very few things that can get every American on the same page, and bringing on a war is one of them.

While assigned in Millington, I was very fortunate to meet another powerful speaker of God's word—Pastor Hardaway. He pastored a church called New Life Ministries, and I must say that I have many fond memories of being associated with them. He was a man full of life and excitement, as well as a practical person to speak with on any issue. There were many experiences that helped to develop maturity in me through the opportunities he provided. Although the church was Pentecostal-based, I was from a nondenominational background, and we had a few disagreements; our friendship, coupled with his love and support of me through many situations, never wavered. He always did and still does present thoughtful words of encouragement to me and makes the time to talk with me no matter when it is or what's going on.

Another opportunity that presented itself has really helped develop me for what was to come. On Wednesdays at the chapel on the naval base in Millington, there was a midday Bible study being conducted by a profound and articulate man by the name of Pastor McGhee. I was introduced into the "fold" by my friend Teresa who had been attending long before I was.

Pastor McGhee not only knew the word from Genesis to Revelation, he also knew it in context and was wise in deciphering its relevance for modern day. He would refer to me as the "Bible scholar" because of my quickness in finding certain scriptures. He was a very genuine person who cared about everyone. Whenever he wasn't able to make it to the studies, he would appoint me to teach in his place—talk about trust and an opportunity! He once told me that it wasn't so much me he trusted but God, and it was God providing the opportunity—I was humbled.

As 9/11 was winding down and I was preparing to transition back to civilian life, there was a change of plans. Being that I had put in so many years active duty in the navy, I decided to return on a full-time basis. So I did what was expected—reenlisted in the U.S. Navy as an active duty sailor. The terms of me being able to do so were that I would come in working with a special program that was considered undermanned. Thus, I chose to come in as an administrative assistant (called Flag Writer by navy terminology) to high-ranking officers. There was no difficulty in adjusting to this because of the fact that I'd worked with officers of all ranks throughout my active duty and reserve career.

The only glitch I faced was finding a high-ranking officer who was willing to accept an amateur flag writer. I was constantly being declined for positions because they were looking for someone who was seasoned within the special program. The special program placement coordinator contacted me and informed me that there was one other unit we could try before I would be dropped from the program. Of course, I was heavily in prayer.

Well, prayer again was proven to work. I was setup with a phone interview with two individuals who would both later become strongly influential supporters of mine—Eulonda and Glenn. The phone interview went very well, and I was accepted on the spot. Once I reported to the unit, my professional growth was all uphill from there. I received unbelievable opportunities to do many amazing things and, particularly, to mentor servicemen and women across all four military branches.

Part of seizing opportunities rests in being sensitive to His leading voice. What I have come to know and respect is that He can use anyone to provide or lead you to an opportunity. Unfortunately, some of us fail to ever get the opportunity because of emotional barriers causing us to reject the one presenting the opportunity. Oddly, some of us will come to find that the opportunity wasn't so much about being promoted as it was about being able to serve. What is significantly or equally as important is the network of friendships He orchestrates to be produced. No one should allow an opportunity of gaining a friend to be hindered by disagreements. Seized opportunities are not times for us to show what we can do but to humbly allow Him to do through us what is to be done. Not everyone must be a Christian in order for an opportunity to be accepted from them—common sense goes a long way when we put indifferences aside.

TIE-IN INSPIRATIONS

~Your actions of today reflect your resolutions for tomorrow!

~If you stop now, you will soon realize that you've never really begun, and all was just a self-inspiring thought.

~Don't allow the judgment of others focusing on how long it's taking you to reach your goal deter you from reaching your goal. What matters is that you have a goal, and you continually progress toward it!

~Being blessed is simply having your eyes opened to appreciate whose you are and willingly sharing His love with others—live life in His peace, strength, and will!

~The rejection of others poured into your life increases God's blessings coming from your life!

SECTION 2

Common Heartaches

IT SEEMS AS though there is nothing worse than having to experience deaths and divorces. They both take something out of you that you may have invested much time, effort, and care in. While there is nothing to eliminate the pain and suffering, He does provide comfort. Too often, many reject His healing method and choose to cope with the emotional wounds alone. He positioned people along our path in life to deliver through them what He is providing to us. We pray why and how such things could happen, but we continually reject His answer by turning away from everyone.

In many cases, the voice of God isn't going to come how you would like it to but in whom He provides it through. Broken hearts can be healed in humility.

~Listen to the voice without looking at the vessel!

CHAPTER 5

Unexpected Loss

IN THE EARLY years of growing up, there were my brothers Tommy, Otis, and Hartzell along with our sister, Anna. We always found ways to entertain one another either in the basement or outside in the backyard—our territories for having fun when not in school.

Maurice wasn't born until 1981, the year we moved to Arkansas. Unfortunately, he would have to miss out on the adventures we were all privy to share among one another during our time in Chicago. We were a tight-knit bunch, always getting into something that would throw our mother into a panicked frenzy.

Anna was the eldest, so of course she filled the role of being bossy toward us and having to have things her way. She would often want us to play "school" with her in the basement as she pretended to be the teacher, and we were her students. I must have been a glutton for punishment because I kept finding myself alone volunteering to be the student just to have her make me stand in the corner for no reason at all.

Tommy, being next in line, was always looking for ways to do something more than we were allowed to; hence, jumping out the bedroom window to sneak to the candy store and constantly getting caught eating whatever was in the refrigerator throughout the night.

Otis was quiet, pretty much keeping to himself, enjoying his hobby of drawing and listening to Elvis Presley as well as being very protective of his "things" and territory.

Hartzell was known for being the curious one, which often led to him getting into various predicaments. As for me, I enjoyed trying to be the selected one (a.k.a. "pick") for attention, listening to music, following the rules, and shamelessly snitching on anyone for anything. (Yes, I was a snitch.)

By the time Maurice arrived on the scene, we were all well ahead of him in age and school. Anna treated him as though he was her child and was very protective of him just as she was of all of us. I believed Tommy to be the major influence on Maurice's life, for Maurice idolized any and everything Tommy had done.

Tommy was such a gifted person with his hands he could fix cars and do all sorts of carpentry without ever reading a manual. The kicker is that whatever any of us could do, Hartzell would come along to prove that he could do it much better; anything from drawing, to carpentry, to automobiles—he was the original "MacGyver" before the television show ever existed.

For whatever reason, Tommy was always the girls' choice. Maybe it was because I was too young for them to get involved with, so since he had my looks, they settled for him instead . . . LOL! Just kidding. He truly was a magnet with the females. More importantly, he was dependable and would give his last, and I can personally attest to both.

There was this one time that a couple of teens were bullying me in the store. All of a sudden, Tommy came in; and without saying anything, they fled. Another time, I was on leave from the military and overspent the funds I had. Tommy, having just gotten paid and taken care of his bills, turned and gave me all that was left from his hard earned paycheck in order to get me back to Virginia. (Well, yes, I did pay it back to him once I returned to my unit and payday rolled around—in case you were wondering!)

Fast forward, the year is 2005, and I am in the military stationed in Washington DC for roughly about seven months. All is going well; I'm settled in and finally became comfortable in getting around the city—most importantly to and from my place of duty. Anyone who has ever been to DC knows how aggravating commuting can be with constant traffic congestions.

All this being said, at about 10:10 p.m. on June 23, 2005, I received a phone call from my mother that one of my brothers is no longer with us. My initial response was "Okay, Ma, stop playing. What's going on?" She then proceeded to tell me the news of something that rocked my world like never before. She stated that my brother, Tommy, had been shot and killed earlier that evening. I'm now in a state of shock and immediately hang up the phone, sat in my room with tears flowing unstoppably. I then called my supervisor and explained as much as I could about my need of having to take emergency leave.

I must acknowledge the outstanding support I received while in DC which came from the group of forty-two navy officers whom I worked with. In particular, there was Captain Tibbetts who pulled me into a room for one-on-one prayer, and well, after the incident, he remained supportive through prayer. Additionally, all the officers provided a collective financial contribution for my brother's children.

To this day, I am forever grateful for all of their support and prayers. Other notable support came from Ptr. Lenard Hardaway and his wife and Ptr. Charles Warman and his wife, all of whom to this day are considered dear friends of mine.

After sympathizing with others in times past, I now found myself in need of something beyond mere words—I needed an outlet linking me to someone who I believed really understood what I was experiencing. I needed a piece of God in the flesh—I needed Him to speak and relay His comfort and peace to me through means of another physical being who could humbly be a conduit of His heart. Not so much that I had questions as to why such an incident occurred but to aid in guiding me through this devastating experience—this place of the unknown that I hadn't really truly experienced before.

What I was seeking came to fruition in the form of four key individuals, one being my mother and the others being the "awkward connections" of a navy captain and two previous pastors. My mother was very instrumental in bringing comfort to the entire family because of God preparing her for what was to come, not in the sense of her foreseeing but her spending that distinct quality time with God to the point where she was sensitive to His voice within.

Days prior to the loss of my brother, she experienced a simultaneous period of uncontrollable weeping with hurt and also an inner peaceful joy that she attributed as God-driven. At that time, she admittedly didn't quite understand what was going on; however, she felt it to be a preparation for the forthcoming devastation.

A principle that I've learned and adapted is the understanding that a "loss" is never a "lost." There is no such guarantee that people, jobs, resources, and circumstances will either remain the same or forever be around. However, when such changes do occur, the issues turn to thoughts of *what about the after?*, *what do I do now?*, and *where do I go from here?*

Thankfully, there are friends and family who God positions in our lives to willingly give the support needed, sometimes in the form of quality, not quantity. Tomorrow isn't determined by our present circumstances and hurts, but it does offer the opportunity for healing, beginning with support from our family and friends.

TIE-IN INSPIRATIONS

~He cares!

When there's hurt, He provides time to erase the pain.

When there's grief from a loss, He provides memories to comfort.

When foolish mistakes are made, He provides opportunity for correction.

When there's a need, He provides favor through the heart of someone to meet the need.

When lonely, He provides company by His Spirit and word.

When feeling overwhelmed, He provides seasons of change.

When wronged, He provides vindication on your behalf.

A faith-walk in Him leads to opened eyes of His provision—the comprehension of His caring!

~Nothing can hurt as much as wishing you had told someone "I love you" or spending quality time with them when there was opportunity to do so. Don't bring this judgment upon yourself by harboring bitterness and unforgiveness—it can only lead to a lifetime of haunting regret. There's time today to squash the disagreements of yesterday. Enjoy, love, and press forward!

~Partaking of God's unlimited blessings begins with exercising proper use of one's limited resources.

-Remaining focused on your future destination leaves little time for reflecting on your past sorrows; however, if you choose to focus more on past sorrows, then you're only left with an empty future.

-The key to conquering fears is accepting the fact that it's He who is within you getting the job done, not you!

-When faced with difficult circumstances and decisions, don't share it with a foe. Doing so will only keep you in the same place or make things worse.

-When the dust settles, remember—through all pain and suffering—that while the enemy would want to cause separation and glory in the confusion, God would design it to develop an even closer bond of love for one another!

-When you lose a loved one, pray for others in grief; when you lose a job, pray for the unemployed; when you lose a home, pray for the homeless; when those most important to you turn their backs on you, pray for the lonely. When you withstand in the midst of such tragedies, it makes room for the grace of God to intervene for a greater outcome.

-Your impossibilities become possible when placed in God's hands and with the proper faith nourishment of surrendering, praying, and trusting!

CHAPTER 6

Asunder

IN DECEMBER OF 1990, it was time for my departure from spending two years on board the USS *Orion* homeported in the great La Maddelena, Sardinia, Italy. What an exploratory and peaceful assignment; I totally loved the area, the culture, and the people.

Anyway, I was permitted two weeks of leave before reporting to my next duty assignment four days after Christmas. So I decided what better place to spend quality time than with loved ones whom I had not physically seen in well over two years—I was Arkansas-bound and very excited!

Upon my arrival, I was greeted with much love, hugs, and kisses. Of course, my mother kept holding my hand as though she was in disbelief that I was really there in the flesh, and my father would carry on with a proud smirk on his face. At the same time, I was absorbing all the attention with much gladness.

The biggest surprise came when I saw how much my brother Maurice, niece Natasha, and nephews Myron and Tommy III had all grown, along with the introduction of my newly born nephew, Dominique. Finally, we were all together again as a big happy family, all under one roof, enjoying laughter and catching up on old-times.

The following day, one of my brothers and I took a ride over to a couple of childhood friends' house, who I thought of more as brothers— Fred and James. (They are biological brothers.) Their mother and my mom were already friends, having worked together for a few years. We shared in a great time as we reminisced on growing up making money from selling soda bottles, pecans, and aluminum cans.

During those times, we were determined kids who went out and conveniently earned money to buy all the snacks we wanted. Surprisingly, I've never had a cavity to this day.

The next day, while at my parents, we received a visit from Fred and James's two sisters. The younger sister had left Blytheville years earlier, was living in California, and was in town visiting her relatives; so in the process, they stopped over to visit my mom. She and I dated, and within a year, we were married. The marriage lasted for exactly thirteen years and produced our two very gifted children, Aubrian and Audrianna.

Of course, divorce succeeded, and we went our separate ways. Next to death, I believe divorce is the most difficult situation for anyone to go through. It has so many trickling down effects, with the major one being the children.

For literally years after, I had constantly beat myself up mentally because I viewed it as though I had given up on Aubrian and Audrianna, although it was far from the truth. Now being in a state of "rebound" and easily infatuated, I carelessly and quickly remarried, and it ended in less than a year.

Talk about what could possibly be worse than one divorce. Try two. (The second was so short it was actually an annulment!) In January of 2006, I vividly remember being alone in my barracks room in DC and crying out to God, my mom, Pastor and Mother Hardaway, and a dear friend named Ken every weekend and every day after work. My mother and Ken literally stayed on the phone with me most of the night, giving me a shoulder to lean on or providing comforting words of encouragement.

If anyone knows Ken, you know that he is the most mild-mannered person who simply loves God. He would always use the word of God to mollify the situation. Pastor Hardaway, a sound man of faith, would say some of the most powerful yet simple words. I can still clearly hear him saying, "Doc, stop wearing your heart on your sleeve and exercise that measure of faith God has given to each of us—rise up and move on!" Although I can laugh now, it was hard to do as he had said at the time, but it was not impossible with God!

The encouraging words by all were well received and did chip away some of the stone that was formed from settling, but for whatever reason, I just couldn't figure out what was going on, and why it seemed as though my life was falling apart. I'll remind you, my brother was killed six months earlier and now a second failed attempt at marriage within a year. Whatever the case, something began to transpire while I was in my room on the last Saturday of January 2006.

While repeating my ritual pity party, I suddenly heard within my spirit the words "Are you done yet?" My answer was yes! All of a sudden, there was this peace that came over me; the tears stopped flowing, and I found myself driving around DC at two in the morning, full of unspeakable joy.

At that moment, I realized two things: I was free from the bondage of selfish sorrow, and the words of those who stood by me served as a jackhammer, clearing away the guilt so that I could receive that word from God Himself!

I was reminded of times past, how I personally and negatively judged people who were divorced and thinking that I was above ever being in the same boat. Finally, humility was knocking, and I welcomed her in.

I distinctly remember when I changed duty locations and returned to Millington, Tennessee, in April 2006, there was a young lady named Lucretia whom I had known for a few years. She came to me with a breathtaking word in regard to the failed relationships that resonate within me this very day; she simply said, "You pulled through like a champ." I realized it wasn't me but Him living within that had renewed my countenance without scathe.

The beauty of this whole story is learning to wait on God. The more I chased after Him, the more He led me away from temptation and delivered me from the evil of the flesh. He has truly protected me from giving in to other "wrong" relationships when I humbly yielded to Him. Eventually, the most wonderful thing happened when I least expected it. I encountered the company of the most amazing, fun-loving, and brightest gift He could've ever created for me—my wife, Ramona.

Knowing that what we all experience is nothing new, including divorce, we must not be ashamed to reach out for help. When help is offered, don't stubbornly to reject it; it could be God's way of delivering a healing answer to you.

Too many times we want God to personally come down and rid us of the hurts and make right the situations. What we forget is that He's allowed it and already there, operating through various people in various ways but all for the purpose of bringing relief and peace. Be grateful for those who give of their time and efforts to comfort you. Not everyone is out to bring you harm. Also, keep in mind when it comes to marriage that if God doesn't put it together, you have an enormous job before you in trying to make it work!

TIE-IN INSPIRATIONS

~Do not allow impatience to add more time to arriving at your answer!

~Do not let your anger lead you to where it takes an act of God to deliver you from.

~Faith takes you to the mountain top, beyond the giants, through the fiery furnace, across the raging seas, over the sicknesses and diseases, around sin, and into the promise of an abundant life—faith is a road least traveled but most rewarding!

~For those who are afraid to love because of past hurts, it is a tragedy to live wasting such a treasure and having to one day answer to God for harboring the gift He has placed in you to share. Don't bill your future blessing with a past charge!

~Having a fruitful life ahead as a believer begins by exercising God's love toward others now! Forgive and love others how you believe God forgives and loves you—beyond all mess-ups.

~If God were to read your life as an open book, would He be credited as the author? If not, allow Him to make the necessary edits for a better ending.

~Praying for a change of heart is surely more effective than fighting for a change in social reform.

~The saddest regret is knowing that you should've listened before you leaped. Getting over that regret begins with forgiving yourself and then asking forgiveness from those whom you may have hurt.

~When someone believes they'll never have a better mate than the one they've had in the past, they're writing the script for receiving someone less. God has a better script written with a more comparable mate in the plan, if one can only believe, exercise patience, and accept it as truth.

~When you find yourself alone and no one to turn to, you're where God strategically positioned you. There were times when you asked to hear from God and were left wondering where He was when you needed Him most. You may have forgotten such a request, but He didn't, and now He has cleared your busy schedule for some alone time with you. Seize this time to pour your soul out to Him—He's listening, and He has an answer for you.

OWEN WATSON

SECTION 3

The Loner

THERE ARE TIMES when doing the right thing will cost you what seems like everything. You begin to question your decision, the loyalty of your friends, and even God's word. As Christians, we sometimes get in a rut so deep that we even question the validity of faith and God.

Through the personal experiences being shared in the following chapters, I've come to realize that, while there are a variety of reasons, some of the most valid reasons of things going awry when you're doing what is right include Him wanting alone time with you, Him dealing with the hearts and integrity of others around you, and Him working a bigger plan that you just happen to be a part of. Whatever the reason may be, I believe that if we remain steadfast in faith and continue doing that which represents Him well, we will share in the position of favor that He has set before us.

~Accept the break with gladness!

CHAPTER 7

Banished

M Y MOTHER ONCE humorously stated to me that there was no way I was going to totally give up the life of being a sailor when that's the only job as an adult I've ever known. She was right because in April 1998, upon being honorably discharged from active duty in the U.S. Navy and relocating from Virginia to Arkansas, I transitioned into the U.S. Navy Reserve and was immediately attached to Naval Support Activity Memphis. The great thing about the Navy Reserves is the flexibility that it offers to serve the nation and yet fulfill your civilian job obligations. It also affords the opportunity for sailors being positioned in select locations for training or for augmentation to other units.

In December 2002, I was recalled to active duty at Millington, Tennessee, in support of Operation Iraqi Freedom. It was with honor and gladness that I served to the best of my ability. It provided me an opportunity to network with other navy reservists and meet tremendous military and civilian professionals. Upon completion of my recall orders, I was honorably discharged in December 2004. However, a month earlier, I had submitted for a prospective assignment to work in Washington DC. Fortunately, I was selected for an in-person interview.

Once I received the notification of selection, I called my dependable traveling partner (my mother) along with my youngest brother, Maurice, and on the road we were, DC bound. It was a great trip for my mom and me, but my brother Maurice was apparently feeling a little homesick— he was on the phone practically 24/7. I doubt if he even remembers the trip or sights we visited while in DC and on a return trip stop in Virginia Beach. At any rate, once we arrived in DC, checked into the hotel, and freshened up, we enjoyed a great dinner and turned in early for the interview the next morning.

The next morning, we awakened, had a quick breakfast, and headed over to the organization where I was to interview. It was cleared for my mother and brother to come along and wait in the lobby while I was being interviewed. In my service dress blue uniform, I must say that I was looking rather immaculate. I was interviewed by a couple of high-ranked individuals, and all went so well that I was selected for the position on the spot. So now as I was honorably discharged from active duty in Millington, I was again placed on active duty for special work in Washington DC with a top organization. Little did I know, a lot was going to transpire exactly eight months from the time I started working there.

The job I was hired to perform served as an incredible experience in being with this organization. The trouble arose when I was selected for promotion to a higher rank. Without getting into all the specifics, I declined going through a voluntary induction. Part of the reason for my decision was based on what a group of us were told—that "unless you go through this process, you will not be known or considered one of us, you will be 'blackballed,' and it will be hard for you to find help when out in the field because we only help one another, not nonmembers."

At that point, it was though my Christianity was being tested to either go with the crowd or follow God. I chose to follow God with the liberty of helping any and everyone, regardless of whether or not they'd been through an induction.

The reaction from the head of the group at this particular organization was anything but "carry on." My choice of not participating had a snowball effect that was rolling full speed ahead and perpetuated by a select group of ranking personnel. Things had taken such a bad turn that I was literally out right ostracized, as junior personnel were encouraged not to have any interactions with me; this was anonymously told to me by a couple of them.

From August to mid-September 2005, I walked alone within the ranks, with very few personnel speaking to me and many treating me as though I was the worst of all criminals. It had gotten to the point that I was told from top leadership that I would not be promoted when everyone else was in mid-September.

For some reason or another, there was an inner peace that encouraged me to stand firm. Well, here's the "but God" moment for you . . . Once the upper management became aware of what had transpired, an all-out investigation commenced, leading to one of the culprits being removed from position; and some of those who complied with the wrongdoing against me came to voluntarily apologize.

Furthermore, the evening of the day prior to promotion for everyone, I received a phone call from a member of management apologizing for the wrongdoing that was employed against me and telling me to be ready and standing in the appropriate attire the next day for promotion.

There are times when you have to be comforted by the peace that He gives you and allow Him to do what only He can do. To this day, I do not fully understand the reasoning behind the entire situation, but I do know that it was a God-guided plan.

All things are not for us to question, especially when you've done nothing wrong and walking pleasingly to Him. It's not the perfect that He's looking to do mighty things through but the humble and obedient. The enemy may start a devastating attack against you, but as long as you remain steadfast, in peace, patient, and humble, you'll see the Almighty God end it in your favor. The family that gets the credit for this outcome is the Father, the Son, and the Holy Spirit—God!

TIE-IN INSPIRATIONS

~Assumption rules a fool's path and leads them to spreading false accusations; whereas truth promotes peace and provides guidance and necessary adjustments for progression.

~Defining and accepting what is right or wrong according to your belief is part of the free will God allows us to have. However, seeking His righteousness keeps you from living a life of wrong and positions you for receiving what He has in store for you.

~Don't resent the push—God is positioning you where you've prayed to be but have forgotten about!

~Doubt provides excuses; faith shows results!

~Faith ignites your being obedient in action, persevering through present circumstances, and obtaining His promise to you!

~Faith is exhibited in doing opposite of what our flesh, peers, or the enemy would have us to do!

~For God to unlock the door of blessings for your future, you must unlock the door of forgiveness for those that have wronged you in the past!

~God's faithfulness is in present time; our faith often relies on future time. A key for receiving is for us to agree with God in the present because between now and tomorrow, our faith can easily be swayed by the pressure of surrounding circumstances.

~Know your battle or become a casualty of war!

~Standing tall is not defined as seeking relevance, accolades or being a bully. Standing tall is simply refusing to bend to the negative pressures of peers, fears, presumptions, and circumstances. Standing tall on the word of God sustains you in serving a greater, positive purpose for all.

~The price of freedom oftentimes encompasses those you thought closest to you, turning their backs on you. In such times, God gives you the peace, strength, and hope for operating in freedom!

~The remedy for hatred is love, for injustice is justice, and for ignorance is knowledge; however, all can only be perfectly achieved by the Spirit of the One and Only God!

~Where and how God leads isn't exactly comfortable, but you will have His peace!

~Wondering how a plane flies isn't as important as you paying the price to fly!

CHAPTER 8

Veiled

IN APRIL 2006, I was reselected for returning to the military organization where I was previously assigned to in Tennessee in support of Operation Enduring Freedom. Once again, I am able to spend more time with my children, reconnect with old friends, and do my part in serving those Navy Reserve Sailors who were being sent over to serve in Afghanistan and Iraq on the frontline.

Upon arrival, for the most part, I was welcomed with open arms as part of the new constructed and expanded team. The administrative processes had gone through quite a change from what I was accustomed to; however, I was able to speedily grasp the new practices with the help of standard operating procedures and a person who would soon become a powerful prayer partner and dear friend of mine, Teresa.

The only hiccup that I had experienced there during the first few months was the fall-out that followed me from Washington DC in regard to not participating in a voluntary initiation program. The backlash wasn't nearly at the level that it was in DC; however, there were a couple of people who made it known that I was not welcomed there or deserving of wearing the promotion attire. My attitude remained respectful toward them as I placed them in God's hand.

In a select branch of the armed services, the standard rule is "Ask the Chief" which signifies being the "go to person that gets things done." Hence, in early 2009, controversy arose and landed in my lap from a couple of junior personnel. Of course, I had to go and confer with God before taking any action, and my one question to Him was "Why did they come to me out of all the others available at this unit?" The answer, confirmed through a friend, was "If you're about doing the right thing for all, why not you?"

So forward I marched under higher spiritual orders. Basically, I was informed by a couple of people that there were biases in how awards and administrative records were handled when it came to certain people. In pulling the records, it appeared to be a fact.

First thing I did was talk to a senior person in management outside of my designated worksite about the issue. She advised me to take it up to my worksite lead supervisor. I wrote out the facts and presented it to my lead supervisor, and he routed it through the proper chain of command. At that point, I was thinking that was the end of my part in this situation; oh, how sadly mistaken I was!

A couple of days later, I was called to the break room by my department head and told that he must inform me that my services were no longer welcomed at the organization because they felt I was creating a "hostile working environment" and that I needed to find somewhere else to go. What a face-dropping shocker to hear that I was the one creating a "hostile working environment!"

Upset at hearing this reprisal for bringing an issue to their attention, I decided to go talk with the legal services office and the investigator general's office. The next day, I was told that I can stay at the organization but will have to move out of the office to another location. I was immediately placed in a massive office in the corner of the building, which turned out to be the visiting VIP's office, used whenever VIPs were in town visiting. By the way, I was placed in that location with only a laptop, no work to do, and alone for three to four months.

During that time, in the midst of an investigation of all the relevant circumstances, I was informed that the awards and administrative records were suddenly being updated. Wouldn't you know it? The conclusion of the investigation resulted in no evidence of wrongdoing. However, I was left shunned for doing the right thing and routing a concern up the chain of command.

Through it all, I was most thankful for the experience because the battle was never mine but the Lord's. What was the purpose of that ordeal? I don't know exactly, but I do know that it provided a well-needed rest. I am very appreciative of those who came by to offer their support and prayers: Jeri, Tony, Mark, Barbara, Teresa, Carolyn, and Marie.

Lesson learned was when people place issues in your hands, be sure to take and place them in the hands of God. There will be many times that we serve as the conduit for God's work in the lives of others. Not all things should have to pertain to you personally in order for you to get involved. Being humble and trusting in Him, you can rest assured that all can and will truly work out in your favor, and God's intended purpose will be accomplished.

TIE-IN INSPIRATIONS

~Don't concentrate on the rugged road you must travel to your destination; instead, rely on the strength of God, adjust accordingly, and remain positive. God knew you could make it; that's why the course was specifically designed for you as a testimony to others!

~Don't spend time defending yourself; it's the enemy's way of robbing you of the opportunity to share God!

~If you sincerely know that God is pushing you to do something that "stirs the water" of the norm, do it as He leads and not by pressuring or criticizing others. Believe that what God is calling you to do, possibly alone, is the start of something greater.

~May each person's purpose count for something positive even in the midst of negative circumstances!

~Most opportunities are missed because we'd like for others to join us, out of fear of doing something alone. Seizing an opportunity (stepping outside the box) could be God's answer for your purpose—you could be the Abraham, Moses, Rahab, Ruth, Esther, or David who opens doors for a greater multitude. Allow your fear to acknowledge faith as the answer—take that step!

~Sometimes bringing about awareness can also subtly promote division and hatred. Matthew 5:43–48 (NKJV) states, "Love your enemies, pray for those who spitefully use you and persecute you, do good to those who hate you, and bless those who curse you!' This enables God to intervene and do what only He can do to bring about change in the heart of the oppressor and clear the direction for the believer.

OWEN WATSON

~There's power in speaking the word of God only when your life is based on living the word of God!

~To harbor hatred because of indifferences is nonsensical; to progress in love beyond the hate is undeniable. Discerning God's voice provides the peace, guidance, and strength needed to press past the struggle and into the promise!

~When God opens the door for you to be the first, don't close it thinking you're the last!

SECTION 4

Laughter

DAILY WE EACH come across something that makes us smile, whether a thought, a situation, or simple conversations. The illustrations of laughter portrayed in the following chapters pertain to the wondrous work of God working through everyday people to reach everyday people. I have no doubt that we've each experienced God working through someone or some situation.

Just like those experiences, the following chapters represent those moments when you just have to sit back and say, "Wow, God was at work reaching and speaking to me through that person or situation." It begins to produce an awesome feeling of excitement when you fully accept that "yes!" He cares that much for each of us, no matter the depths of depravity we've faced, the complacency of where we are now, or the successful achievements we've accomplished. He's yet making moments of laughter in our lives.

~Smile for the camera of life!

CHAPTER 9

The Tender Experience

IT'S 1988. I'D just finished a gruesome but abnormally fun-filled boot camp fresh out of Orlando, Florida, and was now at the end of completing my administrative rate training school at the Navy Technical Training Center (NTTC) located in Meridian, Mississippi. The NTTC was an eye-opener that sort of replicated what it would have been like to be in college. The barracks we were housed in were referred to as mods—having four three-person rooms, each with a full bathroom connected to a common lounge area.

Like being at home, we were each responsible for individual chores for maintaining cleanness. Policies and regulations remained the foundation that kept us focused on a disciplined transformation into the navy culture. Being young, just like in college, there would occasionally be someone to test the waters and have to be reeled in to keep from destroying their future in the navy.

There were only two people that I recognized from my company in boot camp, and at every opportunity we hung with one another as we slowly branched out to make new friendships with others, who either were already at the school or newly reporting. On off time, we would either spend it studying for tests, standing a patrol watch, or hanging out at the base club. I'd spend most of my time listening to music, writing poetry, or occasionally at the base club nursing a cola while observing everyone enjoying themselves.

For those who maintained a high enough grade average, they were granted the privilege of wearing civilian attire and given permission to go off-base into the town of Meridian. During my final couple of weeks at NTTC, my grade average was where it needed to be for me to join in on those privileges.

As our training school time was winding down, we were now all in anticipation of knowing where we were getting follow-on assignment orders as our first official duty station. My two buddies had decided to voluntarily join the submarine community, something I was definitely not interested in or ever considered, especially since I barely passed the swim test in boot camp. However, for them, their follow-on assignment orders were to another school located in Groton, Connecticut, prior to going to their perspective submarine duty locations. For me, the time had come, and I received my assignment orders to the USS *Orion* (AS 18), a submarine tender homeported in a place called La Maddalena, Sardinia, Italy. At that time, I had no idea what was meant by a "submarine tender," nor had I ever heard of this La Maddalena, Sardinia, Italy—I only knew that it sounded like a faraway place and an adventure.

December 1998, I have my uniforms and a small amount of personal belongings packed with airline tickets in hand to fly clueless from Norfolk to New York to Rome, with a final destination arrival in Olbia, Sardinia, Italy. Understand that my environment familiarities consisted of Chicago and Blytheville. Never had I ever thought that I would be going to a country that I'd only read about in text books and saw featured in a couple of movies I may have seen.

To say I was nervous is an understatement, but the need for me to step outside the box served as my motivation that kept me pressing forward. I was convinced that there was more to life than what I'd seen growing up, and I was on a mission to prove just that. One thing for certain, the airport personnel and airline attendants throughout the trip were all very instrumental in assisting this rookie traveler in getting from point A to point B.

Upon flying into Olbia, there were a small group of us who were ushered to a bus that had been awaiting our arrival for transport to Palau, Sardinia, Italy; from there, a ferry would carry us to our final destination. Finally, I arrived to what would be my home over the next two years—the USS *Orion*. At that time, it was the last and only all-male enlisted submarine tender in the fleet.

As I walked up the brow, I was so proud and happy to be part of my first ship and looked forward to the many experiences to come. I personally considered this the first day of actually being in what I considered the "real" navy.

Once on board and introduced to the personnel I'd be working with and for, I went to my "bedroom" which consisted of open-berthing locker-beds (a.k.a. racks) stacked three-high with a curtain, a four-inch mattress, a pillow, and one half-sized standing locker for each person. Oh, and being on the top rack, I had the wonderful view of pipes and wiring above me. I didn't mind it one bit because this is sort of what I had come to picture the "real" navy to be—I actually embraced my new berthing conditions with gladness. Although I did come to realize that despite its outer polished appearance, it was evident that this ship wasn't going to be in commission much longer.

What made this duty station so enjoyable for me was the team we had, consisting of a terrific master chief petty officer, along with the assistant shop supervisor, and then three of us "newbies." The times we all shared were so memorable that it truly made being away from home (and not taking any leave to return and visit) appear as if I were on a short vacation. This is where I learned how to "cuss like a sailor," which didn't last too long because they would all laugh and tell me to leave it to the experts.

As a young Christian, it was becoming evident to others that there was a difference between me and the "crowd." Among those who really assisted in keeping me grounded were two individuals who I consider as my brothers, Antonio and Raymond.

Raymond served as the level-headed family guy who had been stationed in Italy for God knows how long. In the administrative ship's office, where I worked, he was like our father figure in so many ways.

Antonio was the most laid back and even-keeled person to know. Just as I did, he too shared a love for writing poetry. Together we shared in train tours all over Sardinia and a few deployments that were sometimes accompanied by small shipboard fires. While on board the USS *Orion*, I was fortunate to visit locations such as Egypt, Spain, Saudi Arabia, Greece, and the mainland of Italy—loads of fun memories from each place with Antonio.

One day, as I was standing in the ship's galley line for breakfast, out of nowhere I hear this country-style voice ring out the words "Jack Green!" I figured, *No, they must have said something else.* All of a sudden, I hear it again, this time a little louder than last: "JACK GREEN!" I was almost floored to find out there was someone else from Blytheville, Arkansas, who I went to high school with, way over in Italy and on the same ship! It was none other than a childhood friend, Ken.

Before I go any further, let me give you the background on this Jack Green. Jack Green was a cousin of mine and a preacher; my grandfather would always call me by his name.

So going back to Ken, he became very influential in my early Christian walk by reminding me of where I came from (being the church) and slowly persuading me to stop trying to act "hard core" in using language that was unbefitting for a believer.

My thought process at that time was that this was my life, and I am going to live it to the fullest, as long as I am not hurting anyone else. I wasn't aware of how quickly and subtly I began to replace God on the throne with the god of "I." Ken was used by God as a tool to bring things into perspective for me. Daily I began to take note of his Christian walk and how he'd spend his time in the word of God. Slowly, I would find myself in my rack with curtain closed, constantly reading the Bible and writing poems that nurtured the spirit rather than boasting about worldly "successes." There was a change slowly developing that I was eased into by specific persons whom God had in place during His timing.

There are times when you have to venture out to be tested in order to know just who you are and who it is God would have you to be. Your faith can only guide you as far as you are willing to go, but His faithfulness will sometimes press you into far reaching places just to bring you back, refined and stronger than before. The wonderful thing about God is how he uses various people throughout your endeavors to keep you on track. He brings you before that one who delivers His word to you and introduces the life-altering change of His calling. These are times when you can just sit back and laugh in amazement!

TIE-IN INSPIRATIONS

~Doubt says, "But people will laugh at me." Faith says, "But God will bless me!"

~If Christ is truly the King of our lives, we shouldn't sit on the throne telling Him what we want done!

~In being accountable for your actions, be wise in your transactions and stand clear of negative interactions!

CHAPTER 10

The Fighting Spirit

THE TIME HAD come to do a transfer to another duty assignment now that my two-year tour on board the USS *Orion* had come to an end. It's December 1990, and I am repeating the same routine of travel that initially placed me in Italy two years earlier just in reverse. I've received assignment orders in hand and am granted a two-week leave period prior to reporting to my new duty assignment with Fighter Squadron 84 (VF-84) known as the Tomcats based out of Naval Air Station (NAS) Oceana, Virginia. Unfortunately, the two-week leave period at home happened so quickly that I could only remember fragments of my time with family and friends; however, it was well appreciated given that I hadn't been home in over two years.

After all the good-byes to everyone at home, I boarded the plane out of Memphis, Tennessee, heading to Norfolk, Virginia, for reporting to a new unit. I do remember thinking while on the plane that this is what I was born for—being in the U.S. Navy and traveling the world, living the adventure.

My mother would often kid around by telling me that I needed to learn to keep still and enjoy where I am instead of always having to be "on the move." One thing for certain is that I am not one who'd prefer staying in one location long. Even as teenagers in Arkansas, a select group of us would form an expedition group, walking everywhere and exploring the area "just because."

Upon landing in Norfolk and sharing a taxi ride to NAS Oceana, I reported to the top floor administration office of VF-84's designated hangar bay to a surprising sight—everything had been packed and transported in preparation for a deployment to commence within a couple of days. Luckily, there was an officer from the unit who was able to give me a ride out to the ship we were soon to be deploying on, the USS *Theodore Roosevelt* (CVN 71), in support of Operation Desert

Shield and Desert Storm. Upon arrival to the ship, I was in complete awe! If you ever want to witness a fast-paced, energized, and organized environment, I must proudly say that the navy truly represents it, above and beyond.

My first order of business was to locate and report to VF-84's admin office on board ship, and I was very thankful for the officer who guided me along. However, I couldn't get over the impressive size of this ship, along with all the busily moving projects that were going on. The prior ship I was on was only a quarter of the size of this mammoth ship! I'd never seen such a vessel that was capable of housing dozens of planes, housing and feeding thousands of personnel, and was completely equipped with all the essentials needed to sustain a comfortable quality of life for months on end. It was as though my vision and interest in being in the navy had now become magnified beyond anything I could have possibly dreamed of. I automatically knew for a fact that there was no way I was ever going to know practically everyone on this ship like I did on the previous one.

About this time, I am super amped and ready to get my things situated and to meet my department personnel. I tried to portray a "hard-core" nature in an attempt to conceal what I was feeling inside and to keep anyone from thinking I was a novice to ship-life. Finally, I made it to the admin office and met my supervisor, who would eventually have a tremendous impact on my spiritual life—Smitty. He and I connected as though we'd known one another forever. His initial welcoming remarks were done in the voice of Iron Mike: "I'm hysterically glad to meet you!" Hence, the birth of the "dynamic duo." He proceeded to take me around to the various VF-84 office spaces, getting me fully checked in and ready to set sail.

During the deployment, most of the crew on board were assigned to work either day or night shift (being twelve hours). As it would be, he and I were assigned to work night shift. Not only did we have all of our work flawlessly completed, but we also used the spare time as an opportunity to work out, doing crazy amounts of push-ups and sit-ups every night. After all, I had a serious demeanor accompanied with a "minor" cussing mouth, so I needed the physical appearance to back it up. The more we talked all through those nights of working together, the more I began to notice something different about this guy—not once did he murmur any type of profanity. So when I approached and asked him why he didn't cuss, he shyly smirked and said, "I'm glad you asked, my friend, because I am a Christian."

When he made that known to me, all I could think of was Ken from my first ship being reincarnated and transported to VF-84. Shamefully, I must admit that I gave him much push back, using very unkind and unformulated cuss words. He would do nothing but smile and let me know that God is still alive and His feelings aren't hurt. Oh my goodness, I was contemplating about how to somehow possibly go to the day shift—but it would never happen, partly because he had become like a brother to me, and second, he hadn't done anything wrong. He just wanted me to "come to the light." Inside I knew there was a reason for our connection, although at the time I couldn't make the connection.

As time would have it to be, I gradually found myself talking more with him about God and reading passages from the Bible nearly every night, just as I did when I was on my previous ship. It came to the point where he would call me the "hard-core Christian" because of a few select words I would still use and because I was involved in two nearly physical altercations with a couple of others in our office. What I didn't realize at that time was an inward change process that was going on.

That inward change began to manifest in how I would interact with others to the point of becoming the "go-to" guy in the office. Soon enough, I would even get selected as Sailor of the Quarter—for you nonmilitary types, that's equivalent to Employee of the Quarter. For me, this was a grand achievement that became a positive pivotal point going forward with regard to how I would provide customer service in all I did.

Just when you think that your life is fine and all is going well, God reads your heart and tells you what it says through the people He positions along your journey. Being a comfortable or lukewarm Christian is not what He calls us to be. When His call is on your life, He knows when and how to get your attention without offending you—He is the perfect gentlemen! The fighting spirit we each possess is best used when running toward Him rather than against Him. The humor in it all is how He uses people who many wouldn't consider to have the ability to bring about change in someone else's life. However, the many who believe such things are missing the truth. The truth is that it's not in the person's ability but in their availability.

OWEN WATSON

TIE-IN INSPIRATIONS

~Don't count the ignorance of others as shameful unless you have nothing more to learn yourself!

~If you'd like to experience an outpour of God's Spirit, listen to what you say to others that leads to how they view and treat you! If He's truly alive in you, then it's His word that should pour out from you.

~Having common sense in the company of fools is not the same page you should strive to be on. God's intention is not to have your life being summed up by reliving the same page—there are volumes to be written beyond where you are today.

~Valuable friendships are those that you give of yourself to in time, effort, and heart—they're everlasting. Worthless friendships are established on material things (i.e., money, clothes, jewelry, etc.). They perish like snow on a hot day.

CHAPTER 11

Being There

JUNE 1992, THE time had come once again to prepare for another duty assignment elsewhere. As blessings would have it, it wouldn't be too far away from VF-84. As a matter of fact, my new duty station, Fighter Wing, U.S. Atlantic Fleet, was on the same street and about a mile away. For me, this was great news because it meant that I would still able to maintain my companionship with my good friend, Smitty. It also afforded me the opportunity to return for visiting certain other individuals within VF-84 that made life in a fighter squadron very pleasant.

The building of my new duty assignment was an eyesore from the outside. It was in the form of a triple-sized, double-wide gray-colored trailer that could badly use a new paint job. However, the inside housed some of the most wonderful people you could ever imagine. As I entered the building, the first person I met was Rene; she was the commanding officer's secretary. She had a beautiful spirit about her and was graciously helpful to everyone. During my stint there, she would eventually become a great friend and like a mother figure to me—one thing for sure, she certainly exemplified being Christlike.

Just as Smitty and Ken from my past two duty assignments, Rene was another influence that God placed in my path to keep me on the straight and narrow. Whenever I may have done something wrong, no matter the magnitude, I would feel so awkward being in her presence. It was like He was definitely alive in her, but I was hounded by the condemnation of guilt. She was never one to beat me with the word of God but gave of her time in explaining the "why's" and "why nots" and encouraging me to develop the potential within. Rene, along with April who also went through a transformation and who was and still is a good friend, really made being there exciting.

I clearly remember one day that Rene introduced me to this new officer who had reported on board. Being in a rush at that time tending to other administrative matters, I had but seconds to speak to him. The next day, this newly reporting officer called me into his office to assist with completing some administrative paperwork for his checking-in. I happened to notice that he had a Bible on his desk and then asked him if he was a Christian. God was at work again, as he too, was a Christian. There was literally nowhere I could go to escape whatever purpose God had for placing these individuals in my life during that time.

Anyway, we must have talked for about a good fifteen minutes or so when he asked if I'd mind coming to a thirty-minute Bible study after work on Thursdays. Of course, at that time I began bringing out every excuse imaginable in hopes of dissuading the request. When I was done, his answer was "Okay, it'll be held here in the building in the main conference room immediately following work hours. If you can make it, fine." When the end of day on Thursday arrived, I snuck out the back door to keep from passing the conference room and got into my vehicle. Then all of a sudden, something kept nudging me to get out the car and go back into the building. I obeyed!

It turned out to be an eye-opener, as we began going through the book of John from the Bible. The more we did these studies, the more I was becoming attracted to God's word like never before. Eventually my family and I started visiting, prior to becoming regular members of, the church he was a part of—Calvary Chapel of Virginia Beach. Being there really increased my desire for the word and fulfilled God's spiritual transformation in me.

Here we go again. June 1995, I am now getting ready to do another duty station reassignment. As God would see fit, the location is only within a mile from where my current assignment is. I was now on my way to Carrier Air Wing THREE (CVW-3) to spend what would be my last three years on active duty in the U.S. Navy at the time. There were some bittersweet good-byes to all at CFWL, but we were still within close range for being able to visit as time permitted.

The move to CVW-3 was my introduction back to sea duty because, just as with VF-84, we were attached to and deployed on board the USS *Theodore Roosevelt* (CVN 71). What made this tour of duty interestingly wonderful was my late friend Steven Schoenleber and spiritual mentor and friend, Chris. Steve and I were humorously known as Ebony and

Ivory; where you would see one of us, the other was never far behind. Whereas Chris was whom I would refer to as the "walking Bible." Steve and I reported to CVW-3 roughly about the same time and immediately had a connection.

The meeting with Chris was a clear-cut God-send during my final fourteen months there. While on deployment, we both were really looking forward to the Haifa, Israel, port call. Chris, as you probably know by now, was another brother in Christ. Through him I learned a lot of the common everyday aspects of God's word working and being revealed all around us. Disturbingly, many of us as believers seldom take time to appreciate His presence through everyday relationships and His creation of nature. Chris seemed to always have a word that would make you consider how much you thought you knew of God.

As we were nearing the end of a six month deployment, I was coming up on the end of my enlistment contract with the navy and thought I would just reenlist for another term. However, Chris came to me, without ever knowing that I had limited time left on my contract, and delivered a prophetic word that I originally found hilarious. I was soon to find out that it wasn't a laughing matter. He looked me square in the eyes and said these words, "God says that you will be getting out of the navy and going to work for the Postal Service very soon."

That was it, and then he just walked away. I laughed but remained very mindful of what was just spoken. I'd never had any intentions of getting out until it was confirmed through a conversation between my commanding officer and me a couple of weeks later. And so it was! I was getting out and did manage to secure a position with the U.S. Postal Service out of Jonesboro, Arkansas.

Throughout these past three assignments, I was in God's planning process of being prepared for something more—serving others with the tools He had equipped me with as a result of all the prior significant contacts. Sometimes, we can pass up a God-given opportunity by not recognizing His voice and stripping tools that are manifested through other persons or friends. The irony of it all is when we finally understand; He's been at work on our behalf for the longest time! There are valuable friendships and learning experiences that can develop from simply seizing the opportunity of chasing God.

As you've read in the aforementioned chapters, for me it was a gradual nurturing process that led to the strengthening of my measure of faith. Not once was it the "pushy" Christians that drew me closer to Him, but it was those everyday life people who just loved Him and others who served as friends beyond the faith, supportive in the way God would have them to be.

For those who walk suspect of everyone, you're cheating yourself out of what God would like to deliver to you. Wherever you are, you must keep in mind first that you're not there to be happy but to do a job. However, it would benefit everyone if you chip in on bringing happiness to the environment instead of negativity.

TIE-IN INSPIRATIONS

~Don't penny-pinch yourself to the point of death by not enjoying everyday life.

~It's great when others can be blessed from the overflow of your full barrel!

~The compliment of awards declares what others believe about you for a set time; completing your purpose in serving others declares your joy in God for eternity!

~You can't sincerely lay claim to being blessed and highly favored when you're unwilling to share in the lives of others without boasting.

SECTION 5

Life-Living Lessons

GOING TO CHURCH is a great way to stay connected, learn, and be encouraged. The problem arises when people continually leave in the same condition week after week. Is it the church's fault? Probably to some extent; however, I believe it is when we, as individuals, fail to fully yield to Him doing a work within us. Just as there are basic maturity requirements that we follow to live within a civilized society, there are also basic disciplines that we must willingly position ourselves to follow after.

This section is designed to provide general discussions of life-living lessons as examined through the lives of people I have had the honor of observing in their Christian walk, as well as through some of my own personal testimonies. My hope is that you will have clarity in seeing some things in a different perspective and may be encouraged to press forward.

~Better to submit to Him than to live for self!

CHAPTER 12

Forgiveness and Truth

I WILL BE THE first to admit that there is power in forgiveness and truth, far beyond either one being the "right thing" to do. Each, respectively, can either stunt or enhance your relationship with God and others. It's amazing how the failure to forgive and the withholding of the truth can be so evident in one's behavior; they present attitudes of anger, dissension, and evasiveness. Not only are these evident in behaviors that can be naturally perceived, but they also limit the effectiveness of your personal spiritual life. This ultimately results in blanket decision making that hinders the fulfillment of your destiny.

I recall working at an organization and doing a pretty good job; however, unknown to me at that time, my performance was superseding expectations and somehow viewed by other employees as an offense. As time went on, I'd notice how I would perform faster in doing more, whereas they would slow down and do less. The more I evaluated the situation, the more I began allowing an anger to fester within. In my mind, I felt like "why do I feel penalized for making production count while others are getting paid the same or more for doing much less and making a mockery of me?" Now I can tell you that I was wrong in my thinking on so many levels. They weren't the only foes contributing to the negative environment; I had unwittingly become and demonstrated this attitude toward them as well.

While my concern was in making production for the company, as a Christian, I had neglected my first duty in serving people—those around me. I realized that I couldn't blame them at all for something when I had not given the time to converse with them to find out what the problem was. It was then that I had to accept the truth of my calling and ask each to forgive my misunderstanding; what it all boiled down to was their feeling that I was young, energetic, and aiding in management's decision to cut down overtime and possibly replace them—and many had been with the company for at least two decades! When forgiveness ensued and the truth revealed, it allowed for a comfortable, supportive, and family-oriented work environment that we each benefitted from.

As a Christian, I believe forgiveness is a must for anyone claiming to have the love of God within them. A failure to forgive is another way of preventing His Spirit from doing its work through you—this, in turn, results in a misrepresentation of Him. He clearly states that in order for us to be forgiven, we must forgive.

A gauge to know that you haven't been forgiven is the bitterness you have within from not forgiving someone else. Understand that when forgiveness is kept from flowing, it becomes like a clogged sink that begins to harbor anger and resentment so much so that it eventually disallows the natural water from flowing freely through it. Failure to forgive keeps God from being able to pour into a clogged vessel that's clearly unfit for duty. To fix this disruption in flow, there must be a flushing of forgiveness.

Whereas forgiveness allows a flow for use, truth broadens the path for opportunity. Truth sustains a character of integrity and honesty. It is the knock at the door that is recognizable and welcomed by many. When truth is withheld, futures are deterred and so is God's ability to position you where He'd have for you to be. Withholding the truth produces an apathetic lifestyle which makes it almost impossible to maintain a wholesome relationship with any person or organization.

TIE-IN INSPIRATIONS

-Being proud of who you are is not reason enough to separate the colors of the human race "rainbow" that God has made us to be. Striving to work together in harmony depicts a better picture of His will being done here on earth as it is in heaven.

-Faith is a lifestyle—belief and motivation for living; praise is your daily activity—a devoted task; and worship is your attitude—spirit of operation!

-It is not wise to forsake His call on your life and instead think that you are loving God by putting your efforts into attempting to "save" someone who's content and comfortable in doing and being where they're at (no matter how disagreeable their life may be).

CHAPTER 13

Experiences

I'M ASSUMING WE can all agree that mistakes are going to be made by everyone; however, learning from them is what will keep us from becoming repeat offenders. Much like mistakes, the same can be said of experiences we encounter in life. While in church, we all may have witnessed testimonies in which people were either delivered from or privileged to be a part of situations, depending on whether it was something "good" or "bad." In any case, the idea was to have a takeaway that would make one better equipped in moving forward.

In this chapter, we look at a few experiences and attempt to gather bits of inspiration that may serve in making us better representatives of God.

Regularly we'll attend a Sunday or Wednesday service where we hear the powerful testimonies about God delivering someone from disastrous circumstances, sometimes largely brought on by immature decisions. These testimonies are very helpful for the individual in giving God the glory and helping others who may be going through similar circumstances and looking for a way out. They inspire hope, strengthen faith, and serve as evidence of God yet being on the throne and having the final word. But I'd like to bring something else to light, something I believe will equally bring healing, hope, and increased faith. Have you ever thought about people who appear not to have a testimony worth sharing because all seems to be going well in their lives? Or have you ever thought to yourself that the reason you may not have a testimony is because a presumed requirement is that you must have experienced something dreadful?

I am going to share with you something that was impressed in my spirit several years ago, and it was something I do not believe I've heard anyone speak of (at least not to my knowledge). A testimony is beyond being delivered from something that you've gotten yourself into.

There are two other types of testimonies that have been neglected within the church but that I truly believe are relevant. The first type of testimony is what I consider to be "seclusion"—meaning that because someone heard and adhered to the godly wisdom provided by family, friends, or even foes, they never had to encounter the bad experiences that many needed to be delivered from. This type of testimony is based on obedience, and it confirms that God's word is true and that He kept you because you kept His word.

The second type of testimony is what I like to call God-approved. You may now be asking, "Why would God approve a testimony?" This type of testimony is developed when your heart is set on pleasing God, and you are doing everything according to your ability and your love for God, and yet trouble finds you without you looking for it. This type of testimony is not brought on by your "willingness" to experience something for the sake of thinking you can beat the odds. This testimony, I believe, was approved by God so that not only will it bring Him glory and be a witnessing tool in the lives of others; but, for whatever was lacked or lost, because of your faithfulness and trust in Him, He seeks to show His appreciation by pouring favor upon you after it is all said and done. There are but very few who have this type of testimony because of lack of understanding; they begin to fight the battle in their own strength and make void the plan God had in play.

As sad as it may be as believers having to be stuck in our situations, it is even more sorrowful to Him that we lose heart and trust, becoming like everyone else in the world, except we, as His children, misrepresent Him boldly by wearing the "Christian" title of failure. To experience Him at work in our lives should be a privilege that we instantaneously and continually have joy in. Instead, many of us often take for granted His work and His presence in our lives.

Sorrowfully, there is this one experience that is heartbreaking to even discuss, but it must be conveyed. That is the experience of not ever having Him in your life. You go about your daily life passing up the signals that He has planted before you and represent Him calling you. Instead, you allow yourself to be drawn away by your intellect, science, money, and loyalty to certain people or groups, just to name a few. The temporal hurt and pain that we experience is but a grain of sand compared to the massive generations and centuries of people who rejected His existence and the ultimate price He paid for our redemption. Yet He loves us too much to force Himself on any of us; as my friend Mark once said, "God's character is that of a gentlemen who operates with the utmost respect for all."

Lastly, there is the experience of acceptance. Throughout this book, I've shared the importance of family, friends, and foes and how each played a vital role in my hearing the voice of God. That which was really important was me yielding to His calling. If I would have chosen to keep going without ever yielding, just like in traffic, a terrible incident was bound to happen with me being the one at fault. Once I totally surrendered, I have now what came over me that first day—peace through whatever life has before me.

I truly believe that God was using each person mentioned (and many not mentioned) to get my attention. Furthermore, I believe for those who are sincere in their need of Him, He will go the distance to get His message of acceptance to you, and you will have that peace and unspeakable joy that is spoken of within His word.

TIE-IN INSPIRATIONS

~Allowing the Son to shine on others makes room for others to view you in a better light.

~Faith will cause others to perceive you as being a fool but God to reward you for being obedient.

~Living an abundant life is not characterized by relishing in what God has done for you but more so in what He's able to do through you.

~When you fail to share what He places in you, you welcome what you fear and cheat yourself out of what you hope for.

~Being a new creation entails the benefits of:

* The Holy Spirit ushering us through this life.
* A desire for His word in our life.
* Awareness of God being the author of life.
* Being released from the satisfaction of this world.

~When one's eyes are focused on selfish gain in the name of Christianity. understand that the "name and claim it, speak it into existence, etc. . . ." clichés provide the enemy just enough information to dress it up and present it to you as a distraction from what God has planned for you. Better for His will to be done than regretting the acceptance of one's own will coming to past!

~The power of God's love within oneself is conveyed in the treatment of others, whereas the power of one's self is conveyed in selfishness.

~Be not upset or discouraged when you're doing well but others, whom you love dearly, fail to follow your advice or in your footsteps; prayer allows God to orchestrate and implement His bigger plan and purpose for their life instead of your confined plan for their life.

CHAPTER 14

Humility

SOMETHING ABOUT THE word "humility" makes many cringe at the idea of having to apologize or allow another person to have the "upper hand." Unfortunately, many who do exercise humility are often perceived as being no more than weakened pushovers. Predominantly throughout society and as observed in many of the media outlets, you can witness how aggressiveness, coupled with rudeness, symbolizes power and shamelessly warrants respect. What many would find surprising in being humble is that it attracts genuine respect rather than sincere fear; it allows for wisdom to be accepted rather than for poor judgments to be experienced, and it secures relationships rather than not having true support.

I am fairly certain that given the chance to hire between someone who is humble and one who comes across as cocky, the humble one will get the job in most cases. That is, unless it's a job opportunity whose requirements call for aggressive, strong-minded, and possibly rigid behaviors. The trouble with many of those who regard humility as being a display of weakness is that their mentality reveals much about their spiritual life. What it tells is that you may be dealing with a person who possibly doesn't have a meaningful relationship with God and whose heart is in the temporal position of playing God him or herself.

When encountering such individuals, the best that someone as a believer can do is allow humility to lead. You're probably thinking, "Why should I appear weak to someone who doesn't respect the God in me?" Glad you asked. Remember God allows people in our everyday path for a plan much bigger than us getting the glory for a job He is attempting to do through us. When we fail to submit humbly, we hold Him back from stepping in, thus grieving the Spirit of God. We then become the same as the person He is trying to reach by becoming a little "god" who is straining to do the work of the Almighty God. If

I could draw a visual picture of humility, it would be a picture of an upside down triangle encompassing us in the center, X'ed out with words saying "God's got this."

To put a few faces on humility, I would have to look at people in my life that exemplify being humble at a high level. First, my father- and mother-in-law, two of the sweetest and most genuine people I've ever known. I believe it is totally impossible to find a couple comparable to them in terms of going above and beyond with care and concern for everyone, without regard to status. Once you initially come in contact with them, you're pretty much accepted as family (to an extent—because I'm still their favorite, comically speaking). For the most part, whatever they have, they don't mind sharing, and they never glory in personal prestige. Their humility toward God allows the love and favor of God to be effectively expressed through them to all who they encounter.

Another humble person that never ceases to amaze me in her selflessness is a fellow believer and friend named Brenda. She continues to exceed expectations in how she interacts among people of all classes. There have even been a couple of times when she's been deliberately disrespected, and yet she continued pressing forward, allowing God to handle the matter. Her humility opened the gate for God to step in and touch their hearts. Although it may have taken a little longer than expected, those individuals came back and apologized for their supercilious behavior; and of course, she was standing there in forgiveness. Nothing, nor anyone, can withstand the power of God defending His people!

The last person I'll mention is my good friend, Mark. I've personally beheld this guy literally forego reprisal toward folks who were taking advantage of his skills, time, and money. He continually allowed his submission to God resolve all wrongdoings against him. He stands today, not only greatly blessed but also without any scars of regret. He personifies what having a faith walk is by how humbly he carries himself day in and day out in the strength of God. I've come to discover through Mark's experiences how being humble causes you to decrease so that the Greater One can increase, in order to take care of all that is forming against you.

Humility is a key provided by God to open doors which conceal what we're looking for and needing. Coincidentally, it also takes humility to retrieve that same key. The interactions we've become so accustomed to can reach a point of asking who's right and who's wrong. When conversations and attitudes get to that level, rest assured that humility has been completely exchanged for pride. Humility conveys a certain level respect to those who support you, those who you answer to, those who are considered subordinates, as well as those who may be your enemies. As a believer representing God, we must be mindful that there is an order of excellence through humility that allows for God to do His work through us via our interactions with others.

Humility is far from being a portrayal of weakness. Instead, it allows the strength of God to sustain us during those heavy-laden times—those times when others appear to be advancing in wickedness, when we must adhere to the orders of someone who is blatantly wrong, and when discussions go awry in relationships, among numerous other situations. Humility is submitting to His will and allowing Him to step in. I view it like this: whenever humility has to be used, it gives way for God to do something with the situation; but as long as we allow pride to reign instead, we'll receive ungodly results.

TIE-IN INSPIRATIONS

~God positions people to be steered rightly, although there may have been a refusal to listen during years of youth.

~Ignorance offers a failed opportunity to receive a blessing; stupidity simply rejects a blessing; insanity is to view one's self unworthy of being a blessing; sanity is accepting the call on your life to be a blessing!

~Just like living beyond your means, you can give beyond your means as well—avoid the pitfall of unbiblical "guilt."

~When you have nothing left to say, do, give, or learn where you are, move to where God can fill that void.

~Whether learning or serving within a position at church (as a member), know when it's time to move on. God's answer to your prayers of change, growth, and doing greater depends on your obedience to Him rather than your guilt of allegiance. Otherwise, don't pray for such things if you're not ready to put your faith in action.

CHAPTER 15

Serving

DURING THE MID-1990S as a reborn believer, having just gone through some personal issues to the point of walking away from the church for about six months, there was a welcoming call within my spirit to "come back home." The company I connected with was not for my good and was a subtle work of the enemy to kill what had been planted within me. Being in my early twenties and unaware of how attacks occur to distract or deter novice believers off course, the physical man appeared to be winning hands down over the spiritual man. That was until it was made known to me that people at the church where I had attended were in continual prayer for me and had genuine concern about my well-being.

One day I finally surrendered and returned to church. I'll never forget that among the first persons to greet me with open arms was one of the church administrators named Bo. He was a tall blond-haired, blue-eyed "loving Jesus, loving people" type of individual who genuinely and enthusiastically appreciated seeing God at work through people's lives. He exemplified serving in being readily available for whatever job the church would ask of him. Observing the happiness and joy he portrayed in being a well-rounded servant inspired me to not only come back to the church but to get involved.

From that time forward, I volunteered to do church cleaning and took much pride in it. The satisfaction began to develop all the more when I realized that it wasn't so much about me but rather how the service I provided could make life that much better for someone else. Weekly, I would look forward with joy to getting started on my cleaning duties and would often bring my son, Aubrian, along with me. It would typically take about an hour or two, but it was worth it as a character developing task that would later become a standard work ethic of excellence.

That same work ethic would eventually translate over to my performance while employed with the U.S. Postal Service upon being honorably discharged from the U.S. Navy. It had gotten to a point where a couple of the employees were literally offended because of their perception that I was "showboating," while in actuality, it was part of my character development that was orchestrated by God. Interestingly, that gift of serving joyfully made room for me to experience promotion opportunities as a supervisor and officer in charge within an unusually short amount of time since being employed with the Postal Service. That's when it really hit me that serving without expectation and simply for pleasing Him opens up His favor to position you and/or rain His blessings upon you in unimaginable forms.

Speaking of serving, there is individual whom I know by the name of Mark who embodies this characteristic naturally from God's Spirit. I would often laugh when I saw him jumping back and forth between work projects and answering the call for help by others. He makes things happen flawlessly and expeditiously. He definitely possesses a servant's heart in seeking what he can do to make life better for others, exemplifying and uplifting Christ in all he does. With the passion and drive he has, he is known for reaching out to various communities within impoverished areas to provide mentorship, food, and entertaining events. He's a staple in many of the communities and has developed a terrific reputation.

During one specific occasion, I distinctly remember him inviting me to come out and emcee a community event that he and his company were sponsoring. I agreed, thinking it was going to be a few people in attendance due to it being right before Thanksgiving. How wrong I was! I would soon come to learn that there would be over four hundred persons in attendance, and my job was to stand on stage among a gymnasium full of strangers and control the flow of the event. I must admit that a lot of my boot camp company commander's behaviors came into play during certain parts of the program. But as I reflect on it, those four hundred persons were brought together by someone who submitted to God as a humble servant—Mark. Everyone was fed above and beyond and also was given food bags to take home for their holiday meals. By faith, Mark relied on God to open the hearts of many local grocery stores to voluntarily supply the needs of the people—I can attest that God answered in a major way.

Serving is more than just doing; it's an opportunity to illustrate and impart God's work into the lives of others. It's a matter of a heart and spirit humbly being obedient to the will of God. When someone wrongs us or thinks they're "pulling the wool" over our eyes, that is no reason to get alarmed and begin to grieve the Spirit by not allowing Him to do His work through us. Actually, when we do give in to anger to where it affects our serving, that should be a sign to us to determine whether we're doing something based on self or because of a leading by God. In either case, we must be careful not to replace our relationship with God by making "serving" a god. There's balance throughout the kingdom; but in all, there is one priority—His will.

TIE-IN INSPIRATIONS

~As part of the human race of believers called and created by God, we must not forget that we're family and all part of the body of Christ. Therefore, let not indifferences set us against one another as the true enemy would have it to be, knowing that a house divided against itself cannot stand (KJV, Mark 3:25). For if we fall, then havoc shall prevail.

~Being blessed isn't evident in how good you look or in how financially stable you are but in how well you serve!

~Many of us often provide more for the people in the church with little or no thanks in return—as though our giving is something owed to them; however, when we give to those who appear to have no "church" within them and somehow persevere through their daily struggles, they sometimes prove to be the most humbly thankful. Give where it counts—as a blessing, not a "buy-in!"

~Vision Test

♦   Mini vision – "It's all about me."
♦   Small vision – "It's all about my family."
♦   Medium vision – "It's all about my family and friends."
♦   Large vision – "It's all about my family, friends, and people I'm 'okay' with."
♦   Unboxed vision – "It's all about whomever God would have me to serve to the best of my ability and His capability."

SECTION 6

Summary

Family, Friends, and Foes

E VERYONE BENEFITS WHEN they're a part of God's plan. Family, friends, and foes all provide supportive contributions. When we're able to discern God at work through these many individuals, we then humbly become an adherent of His will. The paths He leads each of us on vary and are filled with equipping pieces that can only be obtained through different experiences and people. Letting go and letting God can be useless if we never see God first. I implore each one to walk with open eyes beyond the natural; then we can experience and appreciate the unchartered waters of life as a peaceful journey.

~He's working through them!

CHAPTER 16

Family

MANY WOULD AGREE that family serves as the single most important influence in our maturing, relationships, external interactions, and fulfillment of goals. I view the design of family as God's way of ensuring everyone has a ready-made support system upon entering this world. The job of parenting, though at times may be trying, is vital to establishing a foundation for children to build upon. While it is true that not everyone born comes by way of people who are ready to be parents, God saw fit in using them (not necessarily the circumstances) to get them here—by any means necessary. From the moment we are born into this world, we begin to develop habits, likes and dislikes, and characteristics reflecting those around us.

As I reflect on memories of growing up and visiting my uncle and aunt's house as a youth, I recall really enjoying the times and conversations with my cousin. I was filled with many questions about the entertainment worlds of drama and music, and he would patiently give of his time in providing knowledgeable answers. We would also watch some of those old black-and-white television programs and enjoy some really cool tunes. I still cherish those interactions that shaped me, enjoying what others had to offer in time and companionship.

In today's society, many move so fast with the hustle and bustle of work and achieving personal goals that rarely anyone takes time to just enjoy the simplicity of life and the value of family.

My father and mother both instilled in me the value of responsibility, dedication, and hard work. Although not a person of many words, from his presence or knowing him, you would observe my father's actions speaking loud and clear. My mother is a straight shooter who went above and beyond to ensure that each of us was equipped spiritually and physically for the bumps in life. Having six children to provide for, not one of us ever witnessed either of them complain, neglect, or become discouraged in their well-doing. Neither of them was one to ask for help as long as they were capable of handling tasks together; in 99.9 percent of the time, they did it with God's help. Their committed responsibility went far beyond family alone and extended to the community, church, and anyone in need. There may have been times when either of them may have given their last, but no one would have ever known because they devoted all their work unto God and approached each day in faith.

My wife is the one who keeps me grounded. Not only is she beautiful, intelligent, and fun loving, she also always has my best interest at heart. She is abundantly caring and supportive in all I do. I could write many pages complimenting her; however, to entirely describe her influence in my life is to merely say that besides God, she is the reason for my being a better me each passing day.

My children Aubrian and Audrianna were my daily inspirations as they were growing up. They were the reason for my laying a foundation for them to build on. It is very important that as parents, we do everything within our power to ensure that our children have either a head start or at least are at the starting line of readiness to begin their lives after graduation. Many fail to think ahead and allow their inspiration to be on selfish matters rather than on displaying selfless actions for the benefit of those following behind them.

Family is the cornerstone from which we each find purpose and strength. When that cornerstone is not in place, people become subjected to "live and learn" experiences; and in many cases, this results in an abandonment of purpose. Appreciating the family you have, regardless of whatever disagreements, stress, and dissentions there are, is a symbolic reflection of thanking God. I believe He honors that and releases His favor in one's life to witness the beauty of family and relationships far beyond our natural concept.

CHAPTER 17

Friends

FRIENDS ARE ALMOST as equally as important as family. They often serve as the balancing tool of truth, particularly when family tends to be biased. Friends are the ones who most often go through the painful experiences with you and are more accessible to lean on in person when you're away from family. In short, they become your extended family. They are those who accept and enjoy you for who you are and support you through the ups and downs.

I've had the experience of meeting and developing some great friendships with people throughout my life. God, in His infinite wisdom, already had them ready and set in place as pillars of support prior to the rough patches I've endured and the blissful times we've created. Personally speaking, they are the ones who remained with me when I was ostracized, segregated, needed an ear, or simply needed to be cheered up. They delivered words of wisdom and instances of laughter that can be pulled from the memory banks when needed.

To give examples of a few would be unfair to the many that have impacted my life. Therefore, what I know for certain is that each has made a tremendous contribution to me being who and where I am in life today. I believe each friend to have been strategically positioned by God as an answer for what I needed, not what I wanted in a friend. Recognizing their significance brought me to a place of knowing I was significant.

The value of friends is something that cannot be substituted. They share treasured memories and special moments, sleepless nights, and tears of comfort. Friends push you when you contemplate giving up; they pull you up when you appear to be drowning in woes, and they make themselves available to you no matter the time of day. They are dependable people of integrity.

To be a friend is to possess rare qualities that few embody and have the courage to uphold. They boldly defend you when many stand against you. They serve as a force field, disallowing any harmful weapon from reaching its intended target (you) for the sake of sincere friendship. Lastly, it takes a friend to be a friend—it is a mutual relationship of giving.

CHAPTER 18

Foes

ALTHOUGH MANY OF us detest foes, in hindsight, we can come to appreciate God's permitted positioning of them in our lives. They too were useful tools that helped provide the motivation we needed to move forward. Truth be told, some of those whom we may have considered to be foes actually led to us making vital connections that were valuable sources of support. Others proved to be in place to simply thrust us into our destiny. Too often, many choose to reside in thoughtless self-pity by steadily holding on to damaging thoughts of what someone has done to them, without ever coming to an understanding of how to use that hurt as a springboard for moving forward.

Although at that time I really didn't care for the few bullies I'd encountered as a child, as I grew older and reflected back on the situations, I realized that those were character building opportunities for me. I came to understand that I could have either retaliated by becoming as they were—bitter, mean, and disgruntled—or I could have remained steadfast and allowed God to fight my battles. Even as a child who really only knew of God by going to church, I still had this small amount of faith of knowing He does exist. He stepped in on many of those conflicts by positioning someone else in place to take a stand on my behalf. My childhood friends, OB and James, and my brothers, Tommy and Hartzell, were prime examples of God stepping in as my defense.

There was this one organization where I'd worked and was considered to be the number one employee for two years in a row. Well, when it came time for promotion, I was told by another head supervisor that everyone selected me to receive the honors of the one allotted promotion. I was very enthused to be held in such high esteem, until the "boss" declined me for being promoted. That served as a crushing blow, especially with me working directly for this individual, and he always seemed to be very appreciative of my work performance. I was in limbo and unable to figure out why. For a short amount of time, I resented him and began to question God and others as to how he could neglect promoting me; after all, I was his number one employee throughout the organization, and I'd done all these "great things" to ensure everyone was taken care of.

One morning, a couple of days later as I was driving to work, I pulled over to the side of the road and cried out to God. The answer I received not only startled me but brought a release for me. The answer revealed to me was that my boss wasn't really the enemy as I had come to believe, but he was a tool to show how "I" was the problem. I was seeking favor from man rather than being content in doing my work as unto the Lord. Issue revealed, problem solved, and I was able to move on to forgiving myself for blaming my boss for the issue I had created. Fairness isn't wrapped in someone giving you something because you believe you deserved it. What is in someone else's hand or control, they have the free will to do with as they please.

There was another instance where I applied for employment with a particular organization and was told point blank by one of its human resource specialists that they do not hire my "kind" around that area, but they will go ahead and accept my application anyway.

Learning my lesson from previous experiences, I realized that if God was going to intervene, I needed to be at peace and humbly decrease. So I did just that. A week later, I received a phone call to come in for further testing and eventually got the job. Again, the foe in place doesn't have the final say—we must exercise more faith in God than in the words of man.

This final incident where I viewed the person as a foe occurred again with another supervisor. I was a "by name request" by this individual because of my performance and quality of work from our previous history of working together. There was an issue that arose where I gave a testimony of facts on behalf of some others who were seemingly being discriminated against within the organization. When my supervisor received word of this, he called for my removal. It was a surprise to me, but I had peace inside knowing that this was another enemy-orchestrated attempt to create confusion and division. The decision to sit by and allow God to stand on my behalf positioned me in a much better place. Sometimes, we have to not be so much concerned about what the enemy is up to and rejoice in what God's about to do.

What matters most when it comes to foes is that they are proof that no one is a waste whom God allows into our lives. Some may have true ill will toward you, whereas others are just used to help refine you. In either case, we must be aware that God is involved in these encounters somewhere and somehow, with the aim of making us better and useful for something more.

SECTION 7

Personal Philosophies and Poems of Inspiration

N O MATTER WHAT is going on in my everyday life, a gift that I have been blessed with is that of being sensitive to the surrounding environment. That sensitivity makes way for words to come to mind that offer some sort of solace for going through the trials that people face. Thereafter, I put my pen in action, translating those words into poems and philosophies either on paper or through various media outlets for the masses as a means of empathizing, sympathizing, or simply sharing hope with someone. Today, I present them to you in hopes that you will use them as a reference tool whenever the world around you appears to be cluttered or simply just to remind you of something to smile about.

~Be encouraged!

CHAPTER 19

Personal Poems

Painted Picture Perfect

Faults, I have
Mistakes I make every day
Yet I laugh,
knowing tomorrow's not my yesterday

I go through what others can only
try to imagine and understand
Fashioned as a diminutive piece
in the Master's greater plan

To take the pain(t) away
is to remove the value and pain,
Though we are of various shades
living this life, we all make an influential stain

If lead was used
to mark my legacy's pace,
It wouldn't last long
because the memories will easily be erased

If ink was used
to capture my struggles and fears,
Through my crying, all that would be left are
unidentifiable smears

If chalk was used
to trace the words I say,
It wouldn't last long,
for the rain will come and wash it away

When pain(t) is used
I can never be labeled as a "has been"
Every day brings opportunity
for me to be that portrait everlasting

You see, the canvas may be coarse,
and the frame may not always compliment my fit
But with God as the artist
I can't help but be Picture Perfect!

OWEN WATSON

What the Day May Bring

Wake up in the morning,
quietly lying in the bed
Wondering how this day will go,
juggling so many things in my head

If I get up and make the first step
toward what I'm hoping to be,
This may cause this day to
work out better for me

First thing I do is cast down all
that appears to be greater than my hope,
Leaving no stone unturned,
refusing to get to the end of my rope

Off to start the day
no time for the negative that people say
Surrendering my day's outcome
into the hands of the Almighty One

Regardless of all
I shall steadfastly stand
Rejoicing in His grace
and walking according to His plan

The enemy is busy
doing his job.
I must be attentive and
do the will of my God!

My day is all of a sudden
having a joyous turnaround
My trusting in Him lifts my spirit
For I know each day I'm heaven bound . . . !

Just a Little While Longer—*Rejoice!*

Everyone sees you on the outside
and perceives all is well
Little do many know
the woes you face as though from the pit of hell

You continue on day in and out
making sure everyone is taken care of
Struggling in believing and wondering
if your prayers are being heard above

People distinguish you
as being this amazing person
so they have no thought to ask or offer assistance
rather, choosing to do nothing

Suddenly, a little voice
grabs your attention as you come to yourself
God says he's your sustainer,
by your side, and has never left

What you're facing and feeling
is just something to turn you away
Keeping you from grabbing ahold of your tomorrow
with the weights of yesterday

Maintain your peace,
look not on how others treat you in rear
God has your best interest at heart,
trust and know that your deliverance is near!

Miss You Much!

I've seen you
The life you lived of good and bad
The choices you've made
When emotionally happy or sad
I believe in you
When you often forget about me
Other things take my place
As I'm no longer your priority
I strengthen you
In times of despair when others fail
They give you false hope
Whereas I delivered you from hell,
Although I never change
Nor have I forced you to do my will
It would be nice for us to talk a little bit more
Because unconditionally, I love you still!

Is This Really the "United" States?

If this is the America where all are welcomed to reside
Why is it so difficult to put race wars aside?
If this is the America where all have opportunity to evolve
Why can't we break party lines and truly bring issues to a resolve?

If this is the America that veterans believe in and protect
Why can't we have programs to support them
rather than those that neglect?
If this is the America that we consider as the "Land of the Free"
Why can't we put differences aside and share in prosperity?

If this is the America that swears to uphold and take care of its own
Why are their many on the streets without food, clothes, and a home?
If this is the America built on all being
represented fairly at 100 percent
Why can't all races have equal representation
throughout the government?

If this is the America that prides itself on justice and democracy,
Why can't we do away with those who secure
quotas of incarceration for money?
If this is the America that we're all proud to share of in harmony
Why can't we truly love God, others, self, and country?

OWEN WATSON

You've Got Some Nerve . . . !

To ask ME for advice and still do what you want to do,
Taking MY Word and making it all about you!

To tell others you know ME but act like you don't
When they ask for your help you refuse to and won't

To believe you are meeting ME in a church
but only visit to make yourself feel good
I dare you to really believe I will sacrifice MY holiness
with your complacency of not knowing ME as you should

To sing songs of praise then turn around and dance
to the tune of songs that dishonor me!
Straight from singing "I am a Friend of God"
to "give me a piece of that body!"

To ask how I could allow bad things to happen to you,
when we've never officially met—so sad!
Then use it as a reason to do what you do
as though I will be the one to give in—too bad!

To ask ME for things to satisfy you
yet you could care less about anyone else!
Remember MY second to the greatest commandment is
for you to love others as yourself!

Yes, you've got some nerve
and that's what it takes
For you to come to the conclusion of knowing ME—
Realize it is you who must first break!

What the Eyes See Will Be . . .

Eyes closed
In hopes of escaping the sorrows
Eyes open
Embracing today as your tomorrow

Sleeping eyes
Dreaming of what could be
Awakening eyes
Ready to make those dreams a reality

Crying eyes
Because of painful thoughts
Drying eyes
Now having what you've long sought

Dreary eyes
Hollow of motivation in the life of some
Happy eyes
Having the vision and will to overcome

Frightening eyes
Fear of losing what is had
Joyful eyes
Finally letting go of the past

Eyes closed
A slavery camp for the sluggish
Eyes open
Beginning the work to be accomplished

What the eyes see, *is* . . . !

OWEN WATSON

Better You, Better Me

Looking beyond
what we judge others to be
Taking a moment
to learn about them and them about "me"

Seeing something greater
than we could've ever perceived
Grasping the concept
of what we would've never believed

The same we are
if we all could conceive
A better life ahead
we can surely achieve

Willingly giving
what we each could never get enough of
Is this abundantly free thing
simply called *love*

None living without
realizing how it affects us all
A cohesive family we've become
with heads held high as we stand tall

Hospitality as our persona
just as the way of the south
Uplifting one another
speaking words of life from everyone's mouth

Putting aside differences
with no regard for the poorer or the richer
As we are now a portrait
of a magnificently beautiful picture!

His Joy

Seeing clearly is purposeful
for all to achieve in doing
In a godly direction
we must continue in our hopes of pursuing

He has a plan of action
involving a great life for us in store
Beyond what we could ever imagine
and far much more

The fullness of life
flows through His living word
As we rejoice weekly
Over what we have experienced and heard

He is our God
Mighty and Awesome is He.
Nothing can ever compare
To the extent of His grace and mercy

In this world
we are but passing through
The treasure in us
is sharing His Good News

Wanting for nothing
because He knows our every need
Being there for others
shall we practice and believe

His blessings are you and I
as we are His offspring
Newly filled with joy and love
for the abundant life He's offering

OWEN WATSON

What more can be said
Cannot be communicated through what we speak
But know for sure
it is simply demonstrated by bowing at His feet

You have found your purpose
when you walk within His plan
Relying not on selfish gain
but humbly serving your fellow man

Remaining focused like a soldier
ready to deploy
So is our strength restored
when we realize that we are His joy!

It Is Done!

Thinking back in time
as I relax and reminisce
We used to laugh and talk all the while
next to one another as we sit

The time was short and memorable
so surely I'll never forget
Especially since my emotional eyes were opened
that very first moment we met

Don't dare shut me out now
rather, relay how you really feel
We can't go any further without discussing
and pretend that time will heal

The tides are pushing to batter us
into giving up
Yet the vow we made is forever
together we'll be stuck

I'll seek your smile that
highlights my day
Do what I can to make sure
you are doing better than okay

Whatever it may be,
we need to stand strong and work it out
Not give way to the enemy,
allowing strife and doubt

Look past
what the natural eye can see
Deal with one another in
Love, care, and honesty

OWEN WATSON

The days aren't so bad
as we make them out to be
if only we keep our faith in God and
allow His Word to take the lead

Awaken from your slumber
and put away your selfish pride
You're not walking alone
for I am here by your side
My love hasn't changed,
I accept by faith our future as one
Realizing that the battle is the Lord's,
and it's already won!

Brighter Day

Silly things that make this
world go 'round
Mixtures of various noises
harmonizing a disturbing sound

Be it money or power,
people forfeit their voice
Giving in to false thoughts
proclaiming they had no choice

As bitterness sets in
getting the best of your youth
Memories of past defeats cover
the win of truth.

Every day is spent working
as a busybody bee
Settling for whatever
accepting what you see

Wake up, there is purpose
to satisfy
You still have what it takes
to overcome instead of just getting by

Life can be good
better than the best of any
Look beyond the setbacks
make wise use of every penny

What you have in possession
is a tool to start
Turn the page of yesterday
grab ahold of what'll make you smart

OWEN WATSON

No thoughts of the negative
that others live and say
Use the will of faith
to usher in your brighter day

CHAPTER 20

Personal Philosophies

~A fresh start in life begins with closed lips!

~A friend doesn't have to announce they're there for you; they simply have a credible record of never leaving you alone!

~A friend isn't there to go along with you in your mess but to give toward what makes you better—starting with the truth!

~A friend supports your positive purpose, covers your faults, prays for your strength, and freely gives without having to be asked!

~A one-of-a-kind event occurs the moment you step outside the box and realize there's more to life than the apathetic environment that enveloped you in complacency!

~A true friend isn't defined by the number of associates one has but the quality of a friend one is!

~A truly blessed child is one who can appreciate the priceless gift of God's word instilled in them and guiding their everyday life!

~Although education isn't a requirement to be called of God, you must be willing to be educated and led by God!

~Anyone who blames God for all the wrong in their life clearly thought their works were good enough without God!

~Be amazed . . .

- Not in how someone close betrays you but in how God is always unfailing!
- Not in how others think they're taking advantage of you but in how God keeps favoring you!
- Not in how someone you highly respect falls but in how God positions you to uplift them!
- Not by how much the cost of living is but in how Jesus paid the cost for us to live!
- Not in how you went through so much in your life but in how others can't tell because of the love of God on your life!
- Not in how many times you've failed but in how God continually picks you up!
- Not because you're sort of an unknown among many but in how you are known by God Almighty!

~Be attentive to whom you are assigned and avoid the pitfalls of tending to everyone along the path. Many have become financially exhausted, weakened, discouraged, and distracted because of emotionally driven sacrifices rather than Spirit-led obedience.

~Being called by God doesn't equate to deserving better treatment but employs one to remove self-centeredness and seek God in serving others—a greater level beyond flamboyant words!

~Being stuck on why you can't only fuels the ability of not trying—change the thought, achieve the impossible!

~Believers having peace is so important to God that He has everything written within His word pertaining to what was, what is, and what is to come so that we are equipped against any harmful element of surprises! There is absolutely nothing that should catch us off guard as to why the world is the way it is—for the believer of faith, His word isn't a mystery!

~Building a legacy isn't in how well one promotes financial and materialistic "blessings" but giving of yourself to the greater call of serving others.

~Don't allow personal biases to outwardly contradict your Christian faith—let the faith cultivate change in your heart that will eradicate unhealthy biases!

~Don't falsely blame God for being against you when He refuses to follow you in doing wrong, and now you're reaping the consequences of your choices and actions! News flash—God's not falling for your guilt-trip, nor is He a follower!

~Don't fret about not knowing the plan of God but rejoice in knowing you're in the plan!

~Don't give up on the unlearned, instead teach but do so in love.

~Doubt keeps you being a spectator, but faith keeps you in the race.

~Doubt leaves you looking to be blessed, but faith employs you to be a blessing.

~Doubt leaves you constantly needing a message of hope, but faith secures you with the message of hope.

~Everyone has a song—it's set to the tune of how you live life!

~Faith positions you on the brink of where it takes God to step in.

~Faith is not speaking to receive but living in obedience to whom you believe!

~For many who are called by God, He simply wants you to submit to His will and cease, allowing your dream to become your god. When He's put first in all things, He has this magnificently amazing way of using His purpose for you to bring about the desires of your heart!

~Fulfilling purpose will at times cost you everything but your peace—be not discouraged but forewarned!

~For some, the best that can happen to you begins when someone shuts you out of their life! Let what is over be done, and press into what is to become!

~God can't make possible your impossible when you refuse to totally place it in His hands.

~He is either confessed or denied in how one lives!

~If you see I have too much on my plate, help; if you think I have too much on my plate, ask; if you do neither, you've become part of the reason for what's on my plate!

~In life, we are as kites whereas the breath of God seeks to take us much higher than the strings of man, things, and the enemy.

~In order to be moved by the hand of God, one must first let go of the hand of pride.

~Itching ears require inspiration for self; Spirit-driven believers serve in the best interest of others. Woe unto me if I should achieve all my goals and acquire much wealth but withhold love and attention from others in need.

~It's easier to follow and exalt the titled "man or woman of God" than it is to find one who is actually called and appointed by God.

~Just as you have many friends who are there through select circumstances, you'll always have very few friends who are there for you through any circumstance.

~Many spend their entire lives in church constantly being validated for who they are and never come to know whose they could be. Coming to the knowledge of whose you are empowers one to operate as a servant outside the "church" house, beyond fear, without partiality, and with a love for all.

~One can be taught many things but will most likely repeat what you do!

~Reading and understanding the word of God fine-tunes your ability to hear and recognize the voice of God—you'll come to find out that He's not speaking to as many or saying as much as many are proclaiming He is.

~Realizing you have limited common sense in the company you're with only reveals you are out of your league; the choice is then yours to either smarten up or dumb down.

~Sadly, the best that God has planted within many of us will never come to fruition because we suffocate that seed by continually showing the worst of us in how we live, respond, and treat others!

~Sin can be forgiven without the offender having to ask—it's done through this thing called "love!"

~Stop looking at race and start running the race—God has better plans for our attention and purpose!

~Tell me the truth, I'll listen; try feeding me a lie, I'll challenge you; talk negatively about me, I'll forgive you; assume that I'm ignorant, I'll surprise you; hate me, I'll still love you; try to harm me, I'll pray for you. As a believer, I must yield daily to His Spirit doing the opposite of what my flesh would really rather do.

~The blessing God has for His children is the knowledge of knowing you are blessed.

~The biggest mountain to be removed from one's life is pride; afterward, humility serves as the path to greater opportunities.

~The deal you make with God must be in agreement with His purpose of you!

~The easiest and fastest way to discourage someone from reaching their full potential is to educate them on what they already know.

~The knowledge of good and evil is in what you find comfortably acceptable.

~The more we identify by color, the more we become separated as human beings! Breaking through the color barrier begins by seeing others as being of equal value as yourself.

~The truth doesn't need to be defended just presented!

~There are billions of people in the world, which gives you billions of opportunities to make a positive impact in someone's life beyond family and friends!

~Those against you may know people in high places, but you know the Most High!

- Don't be afraid to live in righteousness, even if it causes others to become your enemy.
- Don't be afraid to take on that new position, even if you're the least qualified.
- Don't be afraid to step out in faith helping others, even if they don't appreciate your assistance.

The Most High has your past, present, and future in His hands, and the outlook is great!

~Those that are not for you can only make your life miserable when you allow them in your life—you hold the key.

~To reject and fight against those that have loved, provided, and supported you warrants the pitfalls before you.

~Today presents an opportunity; tomorrow, you will either have regret or be thankful for the choice you've made.

~Utilizing your gift will take you far beyond chasing your dream!

What you have is all God needs to do something great—it begins by you saying yes and totally surrendering whatever "it" is to Him!

~We strive to do and be so much more for status and recognition that we miss the simplest calling of our purpose by God. This causes many of us to spend more time needing prayer and unable to provide prayer.

~We were created in the greatest image possible—God's image! Sadly, many don't recognize their self-worth and lessen their image by replicating what and who they see rather than on understanding and developing who they truly are.

~What defines a person as being significant or insignificant is found in the value of their contribution to society.

~When you accept whose you are, you then become content with who you are and have no need in wasting money trying to make over yourself to become who others are. You are naturally beautiful!

~When you've gone as far as you can go, trust in Him providing for you to complete the mission.

~When you've truly accepted that you are on a journey through this life to a better life, you don't mind doing and giving your best throughout this life.

~When your giving matches your prayers, miracles happen.

~When your heart is big enough to give pieces to others, God's heart is that much bigger to replenish those missing pieces—don't be afraid to forgive, love, and have compassion!

~When people think they're using you by taking, know that God is using you to give! There's a greater chance that your cup will always be in overflow mode, whereas theirs will continually be empty.

-While you're pressing forward in purpose, it'll soon be revealed that the negative words people have spoken about you are no more than a step in the process; people will later talk in awe-inspiring wonder about what God is bringing to pass in your life.

-Who are you believing—God who cannot lie or man who's susceptible to lying?

-Yesterday's regrets are released when you choose not to relive, remember, or revive them!

-Yielding to Him is evident when you can't help but to make others better by serving!

-You can't build a house on a cloud, nor should you on the words of a fool!

-You're always blessed spiritually, both in the state of where you are and where you're going.

-Your most prized possession loses its value when it is commonly distributed to whomever, whenever!

CONCLUSION

T HE INSPIRATION FOR writing this book has been those family, friends, and foes that have been positioned to share in my journey, placed there by God for a greater reason and a better plan.

What matters most about family is the "gritty" feedback and hard-knock motivation that only they can give out of love. They keep you grounded while simultaneously preparing you to fly, realizing your success is a reflection of their hopes for you.

What matters most about friends is the fact that many can be closer than family. Friendships are developed during the course of life leading to a trail of firsthand witnesses who have supported you through circumstances and the fulfillment of dreams; however, there are usually but a few who have shared with you the emotional struggles and tears of you achieving what had once appeared to be but a dream.

What matters most about foes resides in understanding their roles within your life. Although their intent is to negatively motivate, deter, or hurt you, they indirectly become God's guidepost and tool for positioning you where He would have you to be—humble, faithful, and ready for what's next.

~To all, much love and best wishes for a purpose-filled and successful journey!

CPSIA information can be obtained at www.ICGtesting.com
Printed in the USA
LVOW11*0926210316

479945LV00004BA/18/P